The ISM Strategic Board Series

The ISM Trustee Handbook

ism® Publications

The ISM Trustee Handbook

by Simon Jeynes, MA, BEd

ISM® Mission Statement

ISM is dedicated to the advancement of school management. ISM® provides creative strategies by combining extensive research, proven management techniques, and personalized service.

ISM Advisory Department Mission Statement

Through research, observation, teamwork, and services, we provide each school's leaders with tailored, practical advice and solutions to guide them in building the strongest, most viable school possible.

Independent School Management
1316 North Union Street
Wilmington, DE 19806-2594
Phone: 302-656-4944 Fax: 302-656-0647
Web: isminc.com/bookstore E-mail: pubs@isminc.com

Disclaimer: ISM provides management consulting services to private-independent schools. ISM is not a law firm. No service or information provided by ISM should be construed as legal advice. All Web links and references in this book are correct as of the publication date, but may have become inactive or otherwise modified since that time.

Printed in the United States of America
ISM Consortium member: $69.00 • Non-member: $99.00
Paperback ISBN13: 978-1-883627-01-0
Paperback ISBN: 1-883627-01-X

Table of Contents

Introduction	1
The Trustee as a Parent	5
The Trustee's Role	9
ISM Stability Markers (Third Iteration)	19
What is Strategic Planning/Strategic Financial Planning?	23
Strategic Financial Plan	35
The Board's Mission	41
Tuition Setting	47
Faculty Culture	55
Development	57
Head Support and Evaluation Committee	63
Other Board-Level Committees	69
The Trustee's Commitment to Growth	73
Change	77
Appendices	79
Trustee Workbook	97

Introduction

Being a member of the Board of Trustees for a private-independent school is certainly an honor. You are being asked to take into your care a school, by which is meant the entire student body, to ensure that the education each student receives fulfills the school's mission, and that all students are nurtured and developed in directions that benefit them. You are going to carry out that care by providing support—resources—to the School Head. Your relationship to the school will determine whether your school will be successful in the long term.

Being a Board member is also somewhat puzzling. If you're like many Trustees, you're not quite sure how it happened. Maybe you were approached at a social event. Maybe another Board member had talked to you quite a while ago about it on the phone; you may even have forgotten the conversation. Maybe you were serving on a committee and this seemed the next logical step.

It's also most likely that you are the parent of a student at the school. This makes it more complicated. After all, surely you have a right to advocate for your child, and being a Board member gives you rather more influence to do that. Other parents, in fact, talk to you about their issues as well, hoping that you can help influence the process. In Board discussions, you imagine the impact of your decisions on your child/ren and on your family, particularly when it comes to setting tuition.

Whatever your circumstances, the following two considerations are key as we begin this exploration of what you are/will be doing as a Trustee:

1. You are a volunteer. This means:
    - This is not the only thing you do! Being a Board member is probably no

higher than four or five on your list of priorities (less important than, for example, being a family person; having a career; engaging in meaningful relationships; being involved with your church, synagogue, or mosque; and so on).

- The Board meets relatively infrequently—maybe 10 meetings a year of an average two hours' duration, i.e., about 20 hours. Now, this obviously doesn't include other responsibilities such as serving on a committee, attending events, and engaging in development activities. But the decision-making function that the Board exercises is carried out within a very small band of time.

2. You believe in the mission of the school. If you are a parent, you have seen the power of the school's mission in the lives of your children. You have first-hand experience of the commitment of the faculty and have at least an inkling of the challenges faced by the School Head and Management Team. If you are not a parent, you have a picture of what this school can do for children, in the community in which you live, for society as a whole. You are in agreement with the mission and, without being myopic, you support the school unconditionally. You may know parents at the school and vicariously enjoy their children's successes.

These two key considerations—being a volunteer and believing in the mission—have enormous ramifications. It means that, whatever other roles you may play as a parent, committee member, donor and so on, your role as Trustee is fundamentally carried out in two ways. As a Trustee, you are to:

- support the mission, and
- act strategically to protect the long-term best interests of the school. This is the most important thing to do; you don't have time to do anything else.

This handbook lays out systematically the best practices for this to happen. As you read each section, be aware of your own context, culture, setting, and history, and consider how you might best use these practices in the context of your own school. Each section begins with a guiding principle. This is then followed by a discussion, which is provided with the expectation that you and your Board will consider it thoughtfully within the context of your own school, potentially varying the practice but always maintaining the principle.

It is our hope and ambition that each Trustee who uses this handbook in a proactive, thoughtful way, will be an effective member of her/his Board, enabling it to dynamically support, strategically lead, and wisely steward the school in its care, empowering its students, faculty, staff, and Management Team to carry out their roles with excellence and confidence.

At the end of the handbook is a Trustee Workbook. We encourage you to use this on an annual basis to help clearly identify for yourself what you want to achieve as a Trustee. This supports you in measuring/providing feedback for yourself and for your colleagues on your accomplishments and ambitions for your years on the Board.

A Note on the CD-ROM

The CD-ROM accompanying this handbook contains articles ISM has published relative to effective Board structure and function in its two advisory publications, *Ideas & Perspectives* and *To The Point*.

A list of relevant articles is included at the end of each chapter. It is not necessary to read the articles in order to understand the handbook but, for those who want to get very deeply into the intricacies of any particular aspect of governance, the articles will provide more detail.

The Trustee as a Parent

Guiding Principle: *Once a Board member, and while you are a Board member, your parent role is (in public) subsidiary to your Board role.*

You're on the playground and a parent comes up to you and says, "What do you think of the way the Board has dealt with the dress code?" What do you say? As a parent you may like to say, "Oh, that's terrible. I can't imagine what's got into them!" But you've just been elected to the Board of Trustees. What response should you make?

As part of your orientation, you've almost certainly been given some documents, introduced to the Board President, and thanked by the School Head. You may even have attended a retreat where you all talked about the next strategic planning cycle. Hopefully, you've also been given some advice on how to handle your parent role. The main points might have looked something like this:

1. Although you still think of yourself as a parent, once everyone else knows that you are a member of the Board of Trustees, no one will think of you as a parent! Every statement you make will be treated as if it is an opinion of the Board. The gossip that "he/she said" will now have additional weight given to it. Those who are dissatisfied with the direction the Board is taking will use your opinion to back them up, as will those who are supportive. Solutions that you should consider include:
    a. Only attending functions where there are groups of people, i.e., not getting into one-on-one conversations
    b. Keeping to topics that do not involve Board policy or personality

   c. Politely deferring school-related topics to the School Head or other appropriate school official
   d. Providing a concise summary of the Board's decision and reasons for acting

2. As a Trustee, you will be scrutinized carefully with regard to your opinion of the School Head. It will certainly be difficult at times, but it is critical that your public assessment of the Head's performance be relentlessly upbeat. Your support of the school and its personnel is a litmus test for other parents of the confidence they have in the future of the school. Whatever your private feelings, and however you express your thoughts within the Board meetings, the Head is above reproach. This only changes when the Board as a whole decides that it will change.
3. You must recognize that you now have power in a way that, as a parent, you didn't. You are part of a group that has the ability to close the school, fire the Head, make financial decisions that can affect the careers of individuals, change the mission. Whether you "feel" it or not, your power makes you much more difficult to deal with. Have some sympathy for teachers who appear a little less certain in their dealings with you. Recognize (and appreciate) the care with which administrators couch their conversations with you. Never use your position to exert influence in operational school affairs.
4. You need to be able to advocate effectively for your child. When you approach an administrator or teacher, make them as comfortable as possible by saying something like: "I want to talk with you about Isaac's progress in mathematics. I'm here as Isaac's parent, not in my role as Board member. I want you to know that our conversation will stay between you and our family." From a teacher's or administrator's point of view, they want to know what role you are playing. Some Trustees find it helpful to have their spouse/significant other make advocacy approaches.

Your new role as a Trustee is an important one to the future of the school. Keep a sense of proportion—you as an individual still don't have any real power. The Board operates as an entity and each individual exerts power only as a part of the whole. Stay humble. Keep a sense of humor. Whether you are on the Board for a couple of years or a decade, it won't be forever. And your family is still your more important role. Laugh at yourself a little. Keep a sense of service. It's not about power anyway. You know that. You joined the Board to be able to serve the school with your wealth, your wisdom, your energy. You (should) have no interest in and no part of power politics. Enjoy the opportunity to exercise leadership in this way and ensure that, at the end, there's nothing that you will need to regret, and that the school is stronger because of the service you were able to give.

CD-ROM References

"The Hands-On Side of Orienting New Board Members," *TTP,* 8.10

"When You're a Parent and a Board Member ..." *TTP,* 13.5

The Trustee's Role

Guiding Principle: *The Board has two strategic roles. Each Trustee must support and participate in those roles:*

- *strategic planning/strategic financial planning*
- *due diligence*

The following is a brief overview of the planning and due diligence roles. Each of them is explored more fully in other chapters. Ask yourself how you will use your great capacity to help in each role.

Strategic Planning/Strategic Financial Planning

Every Trustee, including you, must insist on and participate fully in quadrennial strategic planning sessions. These sessions ensure that your school always has a plan that incorporates vision and viability. This plan:

- drives your meetings and committees,
- determines how you hold the School Head accountable,
- identifies how you support the faculty culture, and
- specifies how the Board as a whole ensures financial support for the school.

(See the chapter "What Is Strategic Planning/Strategic Financial Planning?")

❖ One subset of this plan is to sustain the strategic factors that support the faculty culture. Every Trustee, including you, must recognize that it is the faculty who are the intersection of the mission with the students, and that it is the faculty culture which determines the ultimate success of the school. (See the chapter "Faculty Culture.")

- Another subset is the support and evaluation of the Head. Be aware that there is a strange paradox here. The School Head is the Board's only employee. That means the Board must hold the School Head accountable. But the Board lacks the competence to do that! Remember that you are a volunteer with limited time. Think of all the Head is responsible for. It's just not possible for the Board, no matter how talented, to oversee the position of School Head effectively. This task is thus delegated to a committee of the Board called the Head Support and Evaluation Committee. You may be invited to be a part of this committee. (See the chapter "Head Support and Evaluation Committee.")
- A third subset is major gift cultivation. On every Board, there should be at least two or three members who have significant wealth, who have a history of generosity, who give to the school presently, who understand that the school is one of their top two philanthropic responsibilities, and who cultivate two or three others who will do likewise. This is the group that gives leadership gifts to capital/endowment campaigns, provides leadership for the annual fund, and is ready and willing to help the school take advantage of strategic opportunities. You may be one of these people. If you are, become a member of the Development Committee and/or the Major Gifts Committee. If you are not, you will still be expected to support the school financially to the best of your financial ability, seeing the school as one of your top philanthropic priorities as well. (See the chapter "Development Committee.")
- This is all undergirded by the principle that you are mission centered/student centered: You may be uniquely situated in this area as someone who has had children in the school since the school's beginning, has been a member of the Board on and off for several decades, is one of the founding donors, or is an accomplished educator who truly understands what the school's mission entails. Equally, you may just be highly supportive on the subject of the school because of your faith background, or because of what it did for your own child/grandchild. (See the chapter "The Board's Mission.")

Due Diligence

As a Trustee, you are expected to carry out your due diligence roles. These include the following responsibilities.

- Attend all Board meetings. If you cannot commit to attending the Board meetings (assuming that they are set up well in advance), this may not be the place for you. Remember that it is not about you, but about the 100, 300, or 3,000 students whom you hold in trust. They can't afford for you not to be present and concerned about their school.
- Serve on one Board Committee (and no more than two!) and attend all meetings.
- Come to meetings on time and prepared (having read all materials beforehand). Given that each meeting will consist largely of making decisions on strategic items, there will be little or no time for reports. (See "Board Meetings" in the chapter "The Trustee's Commitment to Growth.") So knowing about the school will mean reading the e-mail attachments sent with the agenda, and preparing to make the important decisions that each meeting will bring.
- Stay to the end of each meeting.
- Participate fully in all meetings.
- Welcome divergent viewpoints.
- Demonstrate the qualities of honesty combined with empathy, assertiveness combined with humility, and agreement without compromise.
- Attend school events as requested.
- Contribute (first) to all development efforts of the school.
- Fully and without reservation, support the school and the School Head in public. Whatever you feel about the School Head, any disagreements will only be expressed in the confidential atmosphere of a Board meeting or in one-on-one meetings with the Head personally.
- Completely respect the confidentiality of all Board meetings/deliberations. The Board acts as an entity, not as a collection of individuals. The only opinion it has is its collective opinion. This will be expressed in the form of Board minutes and/or the advocacy of the Board President/School Head. Any individual statements by Board members will only reflect these two forms

of the Board's public face. Confidentiality is thus critical to ensure that all Board members may speak with complete openness, without fear of being quoted/misquoted by colleagues, and always with the option of changing their minds. It also ensures that decisions are not "anticipated" or discussed in the public forum. It allows the Board its privilege of discussing any and all decisions fully and then communicating those decisions in the appropriate way. As in the previous item, dissent is also not a public option. The Board acts as an entity; once a decision has been made in the form agreed to by the Board, the decision becomes every Board member's decision. The only option to a Board member who cannot support a Board decision is resignation.

The following Board Trustee assessment instrument gives you a good glimpse as to how to assess your own performance, as well as that of your colleagues.

Board Assessment Instrument

1. Our Trustees focus on the strategic, long-term impact of issues and decisions.

Rarely	1	2	3	4	5	6	7	8	9	Always

Commentary: Early in every Board-level discussion, the question should be asked, "What is the 'strategic impact' (i.e., impact on the school's long-term institutional viability, stability, and competitive position) likely to be?" For example, if a group of parents lobbies for the addition of a particular middle school sport for next fall, the question to ask at the Board level should be: "Will the enhanced power to attract and retain students over the long run of years and decades justify the impact of the increased tuition (all costs of the addition divided by the number of tuition payers in the school)?" Other strategic questions in this example should include:

- impact on the school's "percent coverage of operations expenses with hard income" (negligible or positive if the math suggested in parentheses above is used);
- part-time versus full-time coach for the sport, and the impact of that decision on the overall quality of cocurricular programs;
- adequacy of facilities to support the new sport;
- likelihood of short- and long-term competitive success in the new sport;

- likely power of the new sport to generate enhanced "sense of community" among the whole middle school student body; and
- congruence (or not) with the school mission.

2. We have developed a planning document (e.g., a strategic plan as well as either a long range plan, an accreditation report, or others) that is simultaneously visionary, practical, and financially feasible.

No planning document	1	2	3	4	5	6	7	8	9	Exemplary document

Commentary: To qualify as a "plan," a planning document must exhibit four characteristics. It must:

- estimate costs for every item;
- show revenue source(s) and revenue impact(s) (meaning for new operations expenses, the impact on tuition) for every item with a cost;
- list the estimated implementation date for every item in priority order; and
- affix responsibility to an individual or to an entity (e.g., Board, administration) for the completion of every item.

3. Each spring/summer, we create our annual Board agenda using items derived explicitly from our planning document.

No planning document	1	2	3	4	5	6	7	8	9	Board agenda derived explicitly from the planning document

Commentary: In the annual cycle of operating a "strategic Board," the Executive Committee annually derives a sequence of Board-level tasks and goals, each of which has its antecedent in the planning document.

4. Our Board is "profiled" (i.e., the Committee on Trustees has created a list of descriptors or characteristics necessary to forward the planning document, and you can see that the Board is peopled by those who have those characteristics—the talents/skills, interests, influence, and wealth—most likely to bring the planning document to fruition), and has potential new Trustees being prepared to join the Board.

No profile	1	2	3	4	5	6	7	8	9	Thorough profiling coupled with profile specific cultivation

Commentary: Each newly developed planning document should spawn a new Board profile. The Committee on Trustees should submit its new profile to the full Board for approval prior to generating names of potential new Trustees. (Note: ISM discourages "constituent representatives" on Boards, for example, the Parent Association President.) The more effective approach is for the Board to proactively initiate dialogue with its constituents, e.g., via the newsletter or speaking to constituent groups.

5. Our full-Board meetings are regularly organized around one major action item on which a vote is taken or a consensus is reached during the meeting.

Meetings not organized on this basis	1	2	3	4	5	6	7	8	9	Meetings always organized on this basis

Commentary: Most Boards have at least one meeting per year in which there is "one major action item" around which the whole session is built. This is the meeting to approve the following year's operations budget—the prototype for all full-Board meetings in the "strategic Board" approach. All Board meetings should be of this kind. Items unrelated to the main item appear on the meeting's agenda, but the clear emphasis is action on the featured strategic item. The allocation of time reflects this emphasis.

6. "Current day-to-day events" discussions do not dominate our full-Board meetings.

Current events dominate	1	2	3	4	5	6	7	8	9	Strategic long-range issues dominate

Commentary: This item concerns the balance that is sought and maintained in full-Board meetings between discussion of current operations vs. discussion of the long-term (strategic) impact of those or of any other issues. Although a particular meeting may need to be devoted to something that is truly "current events" in nature (possibly an emergency), "strategic" discussions and actions should clearly dominate over the course of a year's Board-level work. This is symbolized by the ***lack*** of verbal reports.

7. There is a Head Support and Evaluation Committee (HSEC)—or its equivalent—that assists the Head, when appropriate, in handling "current events issues." This is the only forum for Head evaluation.

No HSEC exists	1	2	3	4	5	6	7	8	9	HSEC operates effectively (handling current events issues and evaluation)

Commentary: ISM recommends a Head Support and Evaluation Committee that, among other responsibilities, serves as a sounding board for the Head and assists, as well, in collecting data that bear upon operations-level success. This committee is the governance/operations linking unit. Many full-Board "current events" discussions are best handled by referring them to this committee for resolution. Note: This committee never meets without the School Head. (See the chapter "Head Support and Evaluation Committee.)

8. Our Board committees are given explicit charges each year.

No charges 1 2 3 4 5 6 7 8 9 All committees receive written annual charges

Commentary: An outcome of Item No. 3 in this instrument should be the Executive Committee's development of explicit, written charges (tasks/objectives) for sub-units of the full Board. Having written these annual charges, the Executive Committee should then decide which committees to create each year. Generally, a committee is created in response to each charge, or to related clusters of charges.

9. Our Committee on Trustees evaluates the Board based upon the Board's fulfillment of its annual Board agenda (which is, in turn, derived annually from the planning document), and the Board takes action on this report.

No Committee on Trustees evaluation 1 2 3 4 5 6 7 8 9 Comprehensive formal evaluation followed up with appropriate action

Commentary: The Committee on Trustees should write a "report card" at least once annually (often biannually), providing "grades" on the Board's success at fulfilling its annual charge, and recommendations for improvement, charge by charge.

10. Our Board has instituted a major gifts program/committee designed to continuously cultivate potential major donors year after year, regardless of when (or if) the next capital campaign is scheduled to begin.

No major gifts program/committee 1 2 3 4 5 6 7 8 9 In place and effective major gifts program/committee

Commentary: The Board's Major Gift Committee often comprises four to five individuals. Only one or two may be current Board members, but each is affluent and habitually philanthropic. The major gifts "program" simply means that each committee member cultivates one other person to the school, its mission, and its vision. When campaigns do materialize, this program is expected to furnish the "lead gifts."

11. There is depth of leadership on our Board (i.e., a number of individuals whom one can readily imagine in the Board Presidency and/or holding critical Committee Chair positions).

No leadership depth	1	2	3	4	5	6	7	8	9	Great leadership depth

Commentary: This item is related to Item No. 4 and implies that the Board profile should always attend to the cultivation of new leadership to Board membership (remembering that such leadership is supportive and capable of implementing your strategic plan).

12. Our Board officers/Committee Chairs are highly respected by all Trustees.

Little respect or respect from or for only a few	1	2	3	4	5	6	7	8	9	Great respect by all Trustees

Commentary: "Popularity" is not a necessary ingredient in leadership, whether the term is used in reference to the School Head or to Board officers and Committee Chairs. "Respect" is necessary, and is usually generated as a result of leaders exhibiting even-handed consideration of issues and focusing clearly both on school mission and on Board-level mission.

13. Our Board places great emphasis on its annual new-Trustee orientation and on its continuing education process.

No education of any kind	1	2	3	4	5	6	7	8	9	Great emphasis on orientation and on continuing education

Commentary: For your Board to operate strategically, individuals new to your Board must actively participate in a well-crafted orientation in which strategic concepts are taught thoroughly and recent Board-level history is reviewed in a strategic context. Only then can new members realistically be expected to become contributors during their first year of service. One commonly used schedule includes an evening session of two to three hours in which the main strategic concepts are taught. This is followed by a weekend morning session in which recent Board history is reviewed, not only in the light of strategic concepts, but also in light of the upcoming year's Board agenda. The ongoing education process would typically be carried out through at least one annual retreat, and through the engagement of association or other consulting expertise to continually develop the Board's sophistication in its understanding of private-independent schools.

14. Our Board committees regularly tap the expertise of non-Trustees, using them as committee members, committee guests, or unofficial "consultants."

No use of non-Trustees	1	2	3	4	5	6	7	8	9	Appropriate use of non-Trustees by Board committees

Commentary: A fundamental precept of "strategic" Board function is that individuals with the greatest expertise in a given strategic area should be cultivated at least to Board committee involvement, and possibly (eventually) to full-Board membership, regardless of whether or not such individuals have had any previous connection to your school. While this is basically a Committee on Trustees function, individual Board committees and their Chairpersons should regularly review their short-term committee membership needs and, when appropriate, submit new names to the Committee on Trustees for its review. (Note: As implied by the language in Item No. 14 itself, non-Trustee participation on a Board committee could take the form of committee member, guest, or unofficial "consultant.")

15. 100% of our Trustees take their "due diligence" seriously (i.e., preparation for meetings; on-time attendance at all meetings; full participation in meetings; personal financial contributions promptly made in support of all fund-raising goals; serious commitment to the confidentiality of all Board matters; and enthusiastic support publicly for the school, its faculty, its Head, and each Trustee's own Board colleagues).

None	1	2	3	4	5	6	7	8	9	100% of our Trustees

Commentary: "Due diligence" comprises individual Trustee responsibilities that collectively make up a cultural "floor," or set of basic, individual behaviors without which no group of this kind can function appropriately. The list shown in parentheses in this item constitutes such a set. (Your Board should feel free to add its own items to this "due diligence" listing.)

CD-ROM References	"Strategic Board Evaluation," *I&P* 26.4

ISM Stability Markers
(Third Iteration)

> ***Guiding Principle:*** *The ISM Stability Markers™, variables that predict a school's ability to sustain programmatic excellence over time, should guide the Board in the strategic planning process.*

The *strategic* role is contrasted with the *operations* role. The first is the province of the Board and the second is the province of the School Head and the Management Team. The Board's job is to look after the next generation of students; the Head's job is to look after the current generation of students. While there is some overlap (see the chapter "Other Board-Level Committees"), the fundamental distinction must be maintained. The research-based ISM Stability Markers comprise the best place to begin in your strategic thinking.

This is the third iteration of the Stability Markers. ISM reconsiders the research at five-year intervals and writes a new iteration in response to the changes (or not) occurring within the private-independent school world. This iteration was determined in 2005.

The item is listed with the corresponding benchmark-placed parentheses.

First Tier in Priority Sequence

1. Substantial cash reserves (20% of operations expense)
2. Strategic plan/strategic financial plan (in existence and in use)
3. Executive leadership (supporting the faculty culture)
4. Hard-income driven (fees covering expenses as close to 100% as possible)
5. Profiled Board (to serve the needs of the strategic plan)
6. Board leadership (depth and succession planning)

Second Tier: No Priority Sequence, i.e., All of Equal Importance

- ❖ Growth-oriented faculty culture (commitment to professional growth and renewal by every faculty member)
- ❖ Budgeted support for faculty professional development (2% of operations expense)
- ❖ Competitive faculty salaries (within 95% of the targeted group)
- ❖ Employee benefits (extensive)
- ❖ Trustee education (ongoing for all)
- ❖ Board/operations differentiation (Board is strategic in orientation; Management Team is operational in orientation)
- ❖ Consistent donor cultivation (following the Donor Cultivation Cycle—see the "Development" chapter)
- ❖ Development Office management (capacity to steward donors)
- ❖ Quality of facility (ability of the facility to deliver the mission)
- ❖ Master property/facilities plan (anticipating future needs—facilities audit—and dealing with deferred maintenance, if any)
- ❖ Internal marketing (recognizing the importance of selling the value the school provides to the current clients—the parents and students)
- ❖ Enrollment demand in excess of supply (wait pools at entry points)

The ISM Management and Leadership Xcellence Formulation

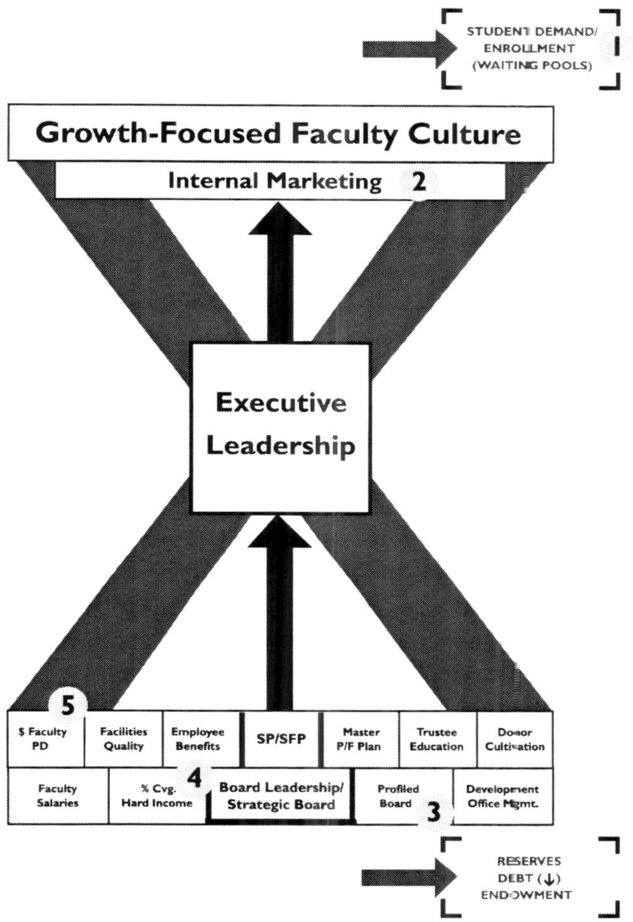

Notes for the ISM X

1. Refers to student demand in excess of supply; also associated with high levels of student performance, enthusiasm, and satisfaction. **Without an outstanding faculty culture (at the top of the X), your school will find it difficult to attract and retain students, much less build demand**.
2. Refers to excellence in internal marketing (specifically mission-supportive communication with current parents).
3. Refers to the process of building Board membership from a determination of the best mix of person-characteristics to fulfill the strategic plan.
4. Refers to the percent of operations expense covered by hard income.
5. Refers to operations budget funding for professional development.

The ISM X™ figure provides you with a graphic illustrating the interrelationship of the various elements.

The base of X illustrates the financial/organizational/structural variables (Stability Markers) that are essential to the long-term ability of the school to deliver educational excellence to its students. This is the strategic province of the Board.

In the center of the X's base is Strategic Planning/Strategic Financial Planning, which incorporates such items as the percentage of expenses that are covered by tuition/fee/investment income (hard income percent coverage), faculty salaries, and employee benefits. The outcome variable for this planning is located at bottom right, below the base of the X—significant cash reserves, lower or no debt, and increased endowment.

Also note the arrow rising from Strategic Planning to Executive Leadership (i.e., the Head and his or her direct reports) at the center. This demonstrates how this planning delivers resources for the School Head and his/her direct reports, which translate into the interpersonal variables at the top of the X.

Let's make it simpler: The Board ensures that the money is there for the Management Team to use to support the faculty in working successfully with the students.

Without such strategic planning, the Management Team (Executive Leadership) is starved of resources, and the financial viability and sustainable educational excellence of the institution is constantly in doubt. Note that the faculty culture at the top of X, with its implied context of student programs, is the operations province of the administration, i.e., while the Board provides the resources for the faculty to use, it is the Management Team's privilege to determine how to use those resources.

CD-ROM References

"The Private-Independent School Headship, ISM X," *I&P* 32.1a
"Management and Governance: The Separation of Power," *I&P* 20.12
"The Third Iteration of ISM Stability Markers," *I&P* 31.10
"The Third Iteration of Stability Markers: A Self-Scoring Process," *I&P* 31.11

What Is Strategic Planning/ Strategic Financial Planning?

Guiding Principle: *A strategic plan is a brief, prioritized Board-generated list of viability-related items to be undertaken in the coming four to six years. The strategic plan is accompanied by a single-page strategic financial plan that projects operational income and expense figures over an equivalent time span, allowing the Board to envision each planning item's financial implications within a realistic financial framework.*

Good strategic plans always have the following characteristics:

1. They are built on a prioritized list of items. Typical items might include the establishment of a cash reserve, the initiation of a facilities audit, or the enhancement of the faculty/staff employee benefits package.
2. Each item is assigned to a responsible person or entity (e.g., School Head, Board Committee).
3. Item implementation is phased in over a multi-year time line (six years).

4. Each item has a cost attached where necessary (the financial resources are needed to implement the item).
5. Each cost is provided with a revenue source (e.g., tuition, fund raising).
6. Tuition-setting each year is based on a baseline tuition gradient—increase—of inflation plus 2% (the increase needed just to keep what you have going).
7. Actual tuition increase is the baseline tuition gradient plus item costs.
8. New items in the budget are always funded at 100% hard income/tuition (unless they are one-time only costs, in which case they can be funded from development income, i.e., solicited income).
9. The strategic plan is reviewed every year (to adjust as necessary) and rewritten every four years for another rolling six years.

Note: Hard income is composed largely of tuition, although other sources of hard income can include endowment and interest income. "Soft" income is composed of solicited income (i.e., donations).

Strategic Planning Detours—Five Examples

You're preparing for strategic planning. As a Board member, you take stock of the school's "state of the union" and note, with pride, aesthetic improvements in the physical plant, well-considered changes in the curriculum, winning seasons for several athletic teams, and other visible successes over the past several years.

You want to continue the favorable growth of your school and harness positive human energy during the upcoming strategic planning retreat. As you approach the upcoming planning session, however, don't allow the momentum of understandably favorable feelings to detour you and your fellow Trustees' process from a truly strategic path. You might, for example, spend excessive time discussing these interesting and positive accomplishments—or give them undue priority when approving items for the plan. Such detours can result in a planning document that is too broad, unfocused, and non-strategic to guide your Board and administration and, in general, to serve your school well in the coming years.

As a Trustee, make it your top priority to stay clearly focused on viability for the future. Is each item to be discussed "merely important" or actually strategic—i.e., specifically dedicated to enhancing the school's stability and solvency? (See the chapter "ISM Stability Markers: Third Iteration.") Keep in mind that strategic planning culminates in a succinct, Board/School Head-created document. This plan identifies the prioritized strategic variables the school must address over the coming five years to sustain (and/or strengthen) its financial viability and ability to fulfill the school's mission.

ISM strongly encourages the financial prudence derived from:

- an accompanying strategic financial plan, which ensures that the plan is rooted in reality by identifying the cost of achieving each of the goals, and
- the disciplined practice of planning to cover all new operations expenses with 100% hard income, i.e. tuition (irrespective of what current hard income coverage looks like).

Note: We believe that you, even if you're not that interested in "financials," must know and understand the strategic financial plan (see later in this chapter).

Detours can undermine these two important financial practices—or bypass them altogether. In preparing for and conducting your retreat, be particularly wary of these five kinds of detours, any of which can distract Boards from strategic focus.

Detour No. 1: Rely heavily on constituent opinion when identifying and prioritizing planning items

What constituents think can matter, but is often overemphasized. It's better not to use surveys at all for most strategic plans. But, if your Board decides to use them, use them carefully! Surveys targeting students, parents, alumni, and/or faculty can be used to ascertain constituent opinion but should be done with extreme caution, and the results should be used only to further illustrate strategic needs.

During your planning retreat, do not allow the survey results to constitute a detour. Your retreat is not the time to bask in constituent acknowledgment of top-rated areas, puzzle over unfavorable results, or seek specific corrective action by way of your plan. Use constituent opinion only if it has strategic implications as you craft and "vote for" planning items: publicizing next-level placement, enhancing internal marketing, or addressing student attrition at certain grade levels, for example.

You may be eager to seek "buy-in" for your plan among constituents and, as a result, over-focus on their participation and opinion prior to the retreat. Keep in mind that, in strategic planning, community support follows from the Board's success in marketing the planning document after it is written and approved. The strategic plan is the foundation and core referent for systematically fostering buy-in—not the outcome of it.

Detour No. 2: Emphasize student programs

When people think about school operations, it's the work of teachers and students that comes most readily to mind. Student programs—the math program, literacy, advising, athletics, clubs, and other activities—can attract significant interest and attention during strategic planning, creating a detour.

Why does it happen? You and your colleagues were students at one time (in one school or another), and many of you may be parents of current students. Add in the engaging quality of discussing student programs and Trustees' personal experiences. Everyone has a favorite experience—being a cheerleader, the Senior Speech, the prom, winning the championship! Additionally, you may be more familiar with public school Boards (and their oversight responsibilities) than with the strategic governance work of private-independent school Boards. These factors can lead some Trustees to see themselves as "experts" in the programmatic work of schools and, even more destructive of strategic focus, see it as their job to plan and oversee that work.

Some components of student programs may, for a particular school, be strategic because they have an impact on the school's market niche (e.g., adding a second foreign language or strengthening the advisory program). More often than not, though, these items are "merely important." As an antidote to the risk of this kind of detour, be sure that you receive (or provide) adequate education about truly strategic variables early in the planning retreat. Make sure everyone remembers that it is the role of the School Head to administer student programs and manage faculty.

The accumulation of cash reserves or the process of developing a profiled Board may not be "sexy" issues (both of these items are first tier Stability Markers), but they are likely to rank well ahead of student program changes as strategic matters for your plan.

Detour No. 3: Become preoccupied with what competitor schools are doing

As with constituent opinion, the external environment—the market in which your school operates—merits awareness. Do not, however, become distracted by trying to mimic what a competitor school across town is doing. Remember the strategic importance of re-recruiting current families by *distinguishing* the benefits students experience at your school and the value your parents receive for their tuition dollars. The strategic emphasis is internal: Make your school strong and distinctive, and market these strengths and distinctions. (Note the importance placed on internal marketing at the top of the ISM X.) Too much external "scanning" can endanger the unique features of your school's particular mission and diminish the quality and amount of strategic attention to the institutional health of the school.

Detour No. 4: Place excess focus on capital items

Like student programs, new or renovated buildings or other large-scale capital improvements can create a detour in a strategic planning retreat. When these bricks-and-mortar items garner too much attention in both discussion and determination of items for the plan, other more abstract but strategic matters—such as Board structure and function, faculty culture, or a major gifts program—may be neglected.

It may be more interesting and, in some ways, easier to picture your school in the future by "seeing" buildings than it is to envision, for example, engendering and sustaining excellence in faculty through daily immersion in growth and renewal, or continuous cultivation of major donors, or more effective ways for the Board to conduct its business. It is, however, the Board's responsibility to be thoroughgoing in identifying the full range of strategic variables (ISM Stability Markers, in particular) that must be addressed in your plan. The "sizzle" and "busyness" of a capital campaign can obscure the real problems.

Attention to these strategic variables, in fact, is a prerequisite to achieve the kinds of fund-raising goals that support capital projects. The more ambitious these projects, the more vital it is to have a planned and implemented strategic institutional infrastructure.

Detour No. 5: Ignore the cost and impact on tuition levels of non-capital planning items

Envisioning a school in the future can be exciting. Long-term, strategic purpose takes priority, however, over short-term enthusiasm. A strategic plan that lacks two components—the cost of the item and the source of revenue to cover that cost (including any impact on tuition)—becomes no more than a 'wish list." Such a list tends to have a short shelf life because, after the initial enthusiasm has faded, it provides little direction and clarity for creating yearly Board and administrative agendas, for setting (and marketing) tuition levels, and, ultimately, for fulfilling the vision of the school across the life of the planning document.

Focus on the Future

As you move into strategic planning, keep the emphasis on components that move your school forward—and beware of detours. Supplement your planning document with a strategic financial plan and, as operations costs are envisioned, address the issue of increasing annual hard income in proportion to increased costs.

Your strategic planning retreat should be characterized by enthusiasm and an affirming view of the school's future. Tempering these feelings with your Board's focused creation of a prioritized set of truly strategic planning items, and a statement about their likely costs, will contribute to a different kind of positive emotion: gratitude for your strategic prudence and discipline on the part of your future Trustees.

An Actual Strategic Plan for an ISM Client

Notes:

1. This plan, being "real," may not follow all the "rules" perfectly. This just means that in every school, including your own, there are particular circumstances that must be addressed. The principles, however, are always upheld.
2. Year One has no costs (and very rarely will have any significant costs) since "this" year's budget has already been allocated. The most common exception to the rule is where an item is funded through cash reserves due to its immediate importance.
3. The base tuition gradient referenced in the text is the tuition increase required in any given year in order to (merely) maintain the current program at its current level of excellence. The measure of this is inflation plus 2%. (See the "Tuition Setting" chapter.)
4. Beginning in Year Two, in the "Costs" column, the annotation $ refers to the percent of tuition increase required to permanently fund this item. Each $ refers to a 1% tuition increase over the base tuition gradient.
5. Note that not all strategic items have a cost attached to them. Often, an action may be one that is organizational or can be accomplished through the use of volunteers (e.g., a Board Committee).

6. Items are typically phased in over a number of years. The Board's orientation is that, over time, amazing things can be accomplished. Being in a hurry is not a virtue.

Year One (2004-05 school year)			
Item	**Costs**	**Revenue Source**	**Responsible Person/Entity**
1. Implement Board governing process through use of this planning document (Item complete)	none	none	Board
2. Initiate a May-to-May agenda-setting process—annual Board agenda and annual operations agenda	none	none	Board President/ School Head
3. Set the Board calendar following the Board agenda and set up Board committees to implement the appropriate elements of the strategic plan	none	none	Board President/ School Head
4. Complete and market the strategic plan together with the strategic financial plan	incidental	operations budget	School Head/ Finance Committee
5. Continue to budget for 100% hard income coverage	none	none	School Head/ Business Manager
6. Build comprehensive statistical database for student enrollment and re-enrollment	none	none	School Head/ Admission Director
7. Search for and hire a part-time Marketing Director (Item complete)	$2,000	operations budget	School Head/ Development Committee
8. Set faculty/staff salaries based on floor gradient	none	none	School Head/ Business Manager

Year Two (2005-06 school year)			
Item	**Costs**	**Revenue Source**	**Responsible Person/Entity**
1. Build a cash reserve of $100,000	$75,000 ($$$/3%)	operations budget	Finance Committee/ Business Manager
2. Set faculty/staff salaries based on floor gradient	none	none	School Head/ Business Manager
3. Search for and hire a part-time Development Director	$5,000 (not extra funds)	operations budget	School Head
4. Review the strategic plan	none	none	School Head/ Executive Committee
5. Develop a Board development outline, including Board education plan	none	none	Committee on Trustees
6. Develop a strategic student enrollment plan including a parent education plan and begin implementation	incidental	operations budget	School Head/ Admission Director Marketing Director
7. Develop a strategic marketing plan and begin implementation	$47,000 ($$/2%)	operations budget	School Head/ Admission Director/ Marketing Director
8. Increase financial aid budget to over 10% from 7%	$40,000 ($.8/1.8%)	operations budget	School Head/ Business Manager
9. Develop a Board profile based on the needs of the strategic plan and increase Board size by 5	none	none	School Head/ Committee on Trustees
10. Implement an evaluation process for the School Head based on the annual administration agenda	none	none	Committee on Trustees
11. Develop a transition strategy for School Head	none	none	School Head/ Board President
12. Use the Stability Markers scoring process to assess progress	none	none	Committee on Trustees

Year Three (2006-07 school year)			
Item	**Costs**	**Revenue Source**	**Responsible Person/Entity**
1. Build a cash reserve of $200,000	$75,000 ($$$/3%)	operations budget	Finance Committee/ Business Manager
2. Set faculty/staff salaries based on floor gradient + $4,000	$4,000 (.2$/.2%)	operations budget	School Head/ Business Manager
3. Develop a strategic development plan for the annual campaign and for major gifts and begin implementation	$43,000 ($$/2%)	operations budget	Development Director/ Development Committee
4. Write and initiate an endowment policy for surpluses and development	none	none	Development Director/ Development Committee
5. Review the strategic plan	none	none	School Head/ Executive Committee
6. Develop a master facilities plan for the development and expansion of the school's buildings and land (Item complete)	incidental	operations budget	Committee on Facilities/ Development Director
7. Set a target of 90% re-enrollment of students and a growth of the student body toward full enrollment	none	none	School Head/Admission/ Marketing Director
8. Assess impact of marketing plan (Item complete)	none	none	School Head/Admission/ Marketing Director
9. Increase financial aid budget to over 10% from 7%	$40,000 ($.8/1.8%)	operations budget	School Head/ Business Manager
10. Continue to implement Board profile and increase Board by 5 (Item complete)	none	none	Committee on Trustees
11. Carry out Board-development plan	none	none	Committee on Trustees

Year Four (2007-08 school year)			
Item	**Costs**	**Revenue Source**	**Responsible Person/Entity**
1. Build a cash reserve of $300,000	$75,000 ($$$/3%)	operations budget	Finance Committee/ Business Manager
2. Set faculty/staff salaries based on floor gradient + $27,000	$27,000 ($/1%)	operations budget	School Head/ Business Manager
3. Carry out strategic development plan	$20,000 ($.8/.8%)	operations budget	Development Director/ Development Committee
4. Develop and implement a planned giving program	incidental	operations budget	Development Director/ Development Committee
5. Review and renew/rewrite the strategic plan; market the plan	none	none	School Head/ Board of Trustees
6. Carry out Board development plan (Item complete)	none	none	Committee on Trustees
7. Increase financial aid budget to over 10% from 7% (10% achieved)	$40,000 ($.8/1.8%)	operations budget	School Head/ Business Manager
8. Complete transition strategy for School Head (Item complete)	unknown	operations budget	School Head/ Business Manager
9. Use the Stability Markers scoring process to assess progress	none	none	Committee on Trustees

Year Five (2008-09 school year)			
Item	**Costs**	**Revenue Source**	**Responsible Person/Entity**
1. Build a cash reserve of $400,000	$50,000	operations budget	Finance Committee/ Business Manager
2. Set faculty/staff salaries based on floor gradient + $47,000	$47,000	operations budget	School Head/ Business Manager
3. Increase financial aid budget to over 13% from 10%	$40,000	operations budget	School Head/ Business Manager
4. Review the strategic plan	none	none	School Head/ Executive Committee

Year Six (2009-10 school year)

Item	Costs	Revenue Source	Responsible Person/Entity
1. Build a cash reserve of $500,000 (Item complete)	$50,000	operations budget	Finance Committee/ Business Manager
2. Set faculty/staff salaries based on floor gradient + $37,000 (Item complete)	$37,000	operations budget	School Head/ Business Manager
3. Increase financial aid budget to over 13% from 10%	$50,000	operations budget	School Head/ Business Manager
4. Review the strategic plan	none	none	School Head/ Executive Committee
5. Use the Stability Markers scoring process to assess progress	none	none	Committee on Trustees

CD-ROM References

"Planning Overview: The Long Range and Strategic Approaches," *TTP* 5.8
"Strategic Planning: The Foundation Process," *I&P* 18.16
"A Sample Strategic Plan," *I&P* 26.9
"Five Detours on the Road to Effective Strategic Planning," *TTP* 10.5
"The Strategic Board: Guidelines for Board Meetings," *I&P* 29.3

Strategic Financial Plan

Guiding Principle: *A strategic financial plan projects operational income and expense figures over the time span of the strategic plan, allowing the Board to envision each planning item's financial implications within a realistic financial framework.*

With a Strategic Financial Plan ...

With this financial document, the strategic plan will be successful because you have taken on the critical step of being responsible for the costs of every item (as needed). This typically means that you have grasped the tuition "nettle" and determined that the school must be appropriately funded by its primary client, the parent.

This document is intrinsically conservative, i.e., it assumes that solicited income (donations) will not rise and that there will be no enrollment growth. While both of these, in fact, may not be true, any changes in those numbers should only be put into the plan after they have been established in fact, not projected forward as a hope. This avoids the temptation to fudge the figures by covering deficits with fictitious increases in these two areas.

The strategic financial plan has the following characteristics.

1. It covers the same length of time as the strategic plan.
2. It is a one-page document.
3. It assumes flat student numbers (i.e., no growth).
4. It assumes flat annual giving income (i.e., no growth)

5. It measures the key components of strategic finances that all Trustees must understand, including cash reserves.
6. Endowment is the least important of the 13 lines (see page 38).

Without a Strategic Financial Plan ...

Without this document, your school invites some or all of the following negative situations.

- The annual tuition-setting exercise may be nothing more than a painful, and often counter-strategic, debate concerning "how much parents are willing to pay." As a Trustee, you may well be one of those parents. The answer to the question is invariably, "Not much."
- The increase in faculty/staff compensation often becomes uncoupled from the tuition/hard income package's upward gradient. Decisions on the compensation package are consequently shaped via another debate framed in language such as, "How much does the faculty need?" The answer, because most teachers are underpaid, is invariably, "A lot."
- The conservative nature of financial documents is overcome by the wishful thinking inherent in most optimistic student recruitment projections. Shortfalls are "covered" by the hope that another 20 or so students will show up.
- The strategically crucial issue of building and maintaining adequate levels of cash reserves, and of continuous attention to their full funding, is often seen as less important or even ignored.
- Trustees think in terms of the current year, not in terms of where the school needs to be in five or six years in order to fulfill its mission in changing circumstances and in order to remain competitive.
- Operations budgeting becomes reactive, not proactive, with the students typically on the losing end.

❖ Accreditation recommendations, almost always expensive and programmatic, are carried out enthusiastically without any regard to their long-term impact on viability.

❖ The school looks to the Development Office as the de facto source of revenue needed to "cover the gap" between hard income and operating costs. This is a fundamentally weak fund-raising position. Instead, this office should be the proactive source of funds to enhance the student's experience (which, paradoxically, will enable the school to attract significantly more donations).

A Sample Strategic Financial Plan

The example that follows is based on the following assumptions:

- tuition begins in Year One at $10,000,
- financial aid is maintained at 10% of the tuition budget,
- enrollment is 400,
- the annual giving campaign currently brings in $300,000,
- tuition is scheduled to increase at 5.5% annually (4.5% to cover inflation and 1% to include strategic items), and
- the Board wishes to build a cash reserve.

Strategic Financial Plan (base gradient 4.5%)

	Year 1 current year	Year 2	Year 3	Year 4	Year 5	Year 6
1A Enrollment	400	400	400	400	400	400
1B Tuition	$10,000	$10,500	$11,130	$11,742	$12,388	$13,070
2A Gross Tuition Rev.	4,000,000	4,220,000	4,452,100	4,696,966	4,955,299	5,227,840
2B Financial Aid (10%)	4,000	422,000	445,210	469,697	495,530	522,784
2C Net Tuition Rev.	3,600,000	3,798,000	4,006,890	4,227,269	4,459,769	4,705,056
3 Other Hard Income	45,000	45,000	45,000	45,000	45,000	45,000
(summer program)						
4 Total Hard Income	3,645,000	3,843,000	4,051,890	4,272,269	4,504,769	4,750,056
5 Operational Expenses	4,000,675	4,180,705	4,368,837	4,565,435	4,770,879	4,985,569
6 Hard Income P&(L)	(355,675)	(337,705)	(316,947)	(293,166)	(266,111)	(235,513)
7 Hard Income % CVG	91.1%	91.9%	92.7%	93.6%	94.4%	95.3%
8 Annual Fund Raising	300,000	300,000	300,000	300,000	300,000	300,000
9 Annual Overall P&(L)	(55,675)	(37,705)	(16,947)	6,834	33,889	64,487
10 Annual To Reserves				6,834	33,889	64,487
11A Total Reserves				6,834	40,724	105,211
11B Reserves Desired (20%)	800,135	836,141	873,767	913,087	954,176	997,114
12 Annual to Endowment						
13 Total Endowment						

Time is Your Strategic Friend!

As a Trustee, you must believe that, for the most part, time is your friend. If you have only a short-term vision for your school, you will constantly be reminded of the inadequacy of the school's funds, facility, program, and even quality of personnel. You will be unduly influenced by crisis and tend to be reactive.

With a strategic vision for your school, you can see how, over one, two, or three strategic plans (i.e., over a 4- to 12-year period) the school can improve dramatically in terms of viability. As a result, it is able to sustain programmatic excellence over time and deliver the mission to students. In one year, cash reserves may seem a pipe dream. Over a decade, an appropriate cash reserve is eminently possible. In one year, enhancing faculty compensation seems totally impractical given all the other matters that require attention. Over a decade, a practical strategy can be put in place to ensure that competent/excellent teachers can be retained and recruited far into the school's future.

The importance of time cannot be overestimated. As a Trustee, being concerned for the well-being of the current students' children (your grandchildren) enables you to take a measured and disciplined view of the school's progress. So, two important characteristics you must demonstrate (whether they are "natural" to you or not) are:

- **patience**: it doesn't have to happen tomorrow, despite what all non-Trustees might wish for; and
- **fiscal discipline**: objectives must be prioritized according to their impact on viability and worked on systematically (e.g., cash reserves before endowment).

CD-ROM References

"The Board and Your School's Strategic Financial Plan," *TTP* 13.8
"A Line-by-Line Guide to Developing a Strategic Financial Plan," *TTP* 13.8
"The Strategic Financial Plan: a Checklist for Trustees," *I&P* 22.15
"Your Strategic Financial Plan: Format and Reporting," *I&P* 28.9

The Board's Mission

> ***Guiding Principle:*** *The Board's mission is to support the mission of the school by taking viability-focused action on behalf of the next generation of students.*

Now that we understand the nature of your job, it's time to talk about mission. On the one hand, it is a truism that Trustees support the mission of the school and have it as a part of their "trust." On the other hand, that can lead you to believe that, to fulfill that role, you have to know what's going on in the school, in each classroom, in the curriculum, and with each faculty member. You may feel that the School Head should be giving a report at every Board meeting about the state of the school, and that you should be fundamentally concerned with these matters. Nothing is further from the truth!

You hired the School Head to handle those operational matters. Your job is to support the School Head through your strategic role and exercise your own due diligence. To make sure you understand your relationship to the school mission in the right way, ensure that your Board has its own mission statement.

In ISM's experience, most Boards have not taken this step. Sometimes, it's because they didn't think of it. Other times, it's because mission seems like a vague kind of thing with little practical application. In other cases, it's because the individual Trustees could not agree on the Board's fundamental mission. If you don't have a Board mission statement, develop one with the following thoughts in mind. If you do have one, reconsider it based on these principles.

While mission statements can, indeed, be vague and not very useful, the one we provide as a template (see the Guiding Principle for this chapter) is very clear about how the Board should be going about its business.

- The Board is to support the mission of the school, not in the sense of opposing all change, but in the sense of ensuring the following.
  - The mission is always central to decision making—how does a plan of action support or not support the mission?
  - The mission is an ongoing process. What does the mission mean in new circumstances (e.g., the word "family" in 1950 was a very narrow term; in 2007, it encompasses a wide number of relationships).
  - The mission must continue to develop. As a Trustee, encourage a revisiting of the mission statement every eight years and whenever major changes or events occur—a building project is completed, the student population increases or decreases dramatically, the program changes, or the school goes through an accreditation process.
- The Board is charged with taking viability-related action, which means very bluntly that you must ensure that the school (Management Team) has the resources it needs to carry out the mission in the life of its students—money, facilities, support for programs, enough administrators, public affirmation of the school, and so on.
- Financially, the Board's important roles include setting tuition, donating money, soliciting donations from others, renewing and building facilities, and setting the budget.
- The Board is to take such actions to benefit not the current students, but the children of the current students with the following implications.
  - It is conceivable that the results of the actions taken will not be fully (or even largely) realized in the time you are on the Board. Examples might include the attempt to improve faculty compensation over time (with a 10-year time line), or the desire to build endowment (with a 50-year time line).
  - It is conceivable that you will allow a current dilemma to go unresolved because it is part of a broader issue. For example, the lack of air-conditioning in a classroom may continue as you develop a master

facilities plan that will enable the Board to deal with the situation in a far more permanent and effective fashion.

- It is also conceivable that you will take direct action to solve a "now" problem because it is also a future problem. For example, you might support the faculty (at the School Head's request) by increasing the academic budget line in order to renew the entire social studies and science textbook collections on an ongoing basis.

The power of the Board's mission statement is that the conversation is always brought back to the basic question: What are you here for? The mission statement answers that question: We're here to support the school mission, ensuring that our actions are always student-centered and have a future orientation.

Strategic Versus Operations: What's the Difference?

Let's revisit this topic. When Boards stray into the operational realm, the result is almost always bad for the school. If they stay in the strategic realm and act in a mission-appropriate way, it's almost always good for the school.

What's the bridge between strategicness and operations? The School Head! That's the top reason why the relationship between the Board of Trustees and the School Head is critical. One of the ways to ensure that it stays healthy is to constantly monitor the separation of strategic responsibilities and operations responsibilities. The following table gives a sample of what this can look like.

Are there gray areas? Yes, nothing is ever quite as clear as we might like it. Marketing is really an operations responsibility, but many Boards have Marketing Committees to put together strategic marketing plans and ensure the school has the resources to implement them. Facilities is definitely operational, but often requires significant funds to, for example, look after deferred maintenance. Development is strategic and operational: The annual fund is usually run by the Director of Development—an operations function—while capital campaigns are typically run from the Board level with support from the school's Development Office.

Don't sweat the perfect answer. Ensure that whatever the Board is looking after has a strategic importance, while ensuring that the School Head is given the autonomy to actually carry out the activity.

Strategic Responsibilities (Board)	Responsibilities (School Head)
School mission (approval of any mission/philosophy statements)	School mission (day-to-day application)
Strategic plan	Definition of Professional Excellence*
Strategic financial plan	Portrait of the Graduate*
Annual agenda	Annual administration agenda
School Head evaluation, hiring, and firing	Faculty and staff evaluation, hiring, and firing
Budget (broad categories) and tuition setting	Budget—how the money is allocated and disbursed line by line
Facilities planning, construction, renovation	Facilities maintenance
Master campus development plan	Facilities audit
Marketing plan/parent retention and education plan	Marketing plan/parent retention and education plan implementation
	Curriculum—content, how it's taught, and materials used
Leadership in development	Development Office management
Major gifts	Annual fund
Appropriate funding of professional development	Establishing a growth-focused faculty culture

* See "Purpose and Outcome Statements" in this chapter.

Purpose and Outcome Statements

The three items that make up your school's Purpose and Outcome Statements—the mission statement, the Portrait of the Graduate, and the Characteristics of Professional Excellence—provide the foundation for:

- capturing the essence of a school;
- distinguishing it from other schools;

- providing guidance to the Board, administration, and faculty in their pursuit of programmatic excellence; and
- answering the essential question, "Why does our school exist?"

❖ **Mission statement.** While a mission statement is valuable, it is frequently inadequate—no matter how beautiful the wording. This is an attempt to capture, in 30 words or less, the core reasons your school exists and the programs and qualities that set it apart. Over the years, ISM has found that private-independent school mission statements are seldom viewed as completely satisfactory by any constituent group, whether it be the faculty and staff, the administration, the parent body, alumni, or others with an interest in the school (e.g., prospective lead donors).

❖ **Portrait of the Graduate.** Outside of the educational attainments of your graduates, what other distinguishing characteristics do they have which are, at least in part, a result of the years they spent at your school? This portrait can be tested as you stay in communication with your alumni over the years.

❖ **Characteristics of Professional Excellence.** This statement is created by the faculty and describes, ideally, what the mission looks like in the daily words and actions (reflecting attitudes and behaviors) of each teacher. This can help identify strengths and weaknesses in the faculty culture and enable the Academic Management Team, together with the teachers, to discuss and take appropriate steps.

The action element that energizes and provides a foundation for these statements is a strategic plan/strategic financial plan—the plan for your school's near-term future, and the financial plan that serves as the "fuel" to support its completion.

CD-ROM References

"The Board Mission Statement," *TTP* 13.3

Tuition Setting

Guiding Principle: *Tuition setting is about mission, not really about money at all. Tuition represents the cost of what the Board wants the school to be in order to deliver its mission, divided by the number of students.**

Tuition setting is one of the Board's most difficult tasks. As an individual Board member, particularly if you are a parent, talking about tuition (which you must do every year) can often be an exercise in frustration. Typical questions arise.

- ❖ How much did we raise tuition last year?
- ❖ How much does the competition charge?
- ❖ What can parents afford/are they willing to pay?
- ❖ What do you think our fund raising can produce?
- ❖ How do we keep our school affordable?

The simple answer is that none of these questions really matter, or at least they matter a lot less than this most strategic question: *Given our mission, what kind of education (and at what level of excellence) do we want to provide for our students?*

From a Board member's perspective, you must approach tuition setting from a strategic/mission point of view. This means the following steps must be taken.

1. Develop a strategic plan. This will answer the question about how to sustain (and maybe improve) the excellence of the education being provided to the students.
2. Develop the accompanying strategic financial plan. This will tell you what the plan costs.
3. Market both to your "client." This respects the parent in the marketplace, creates transparency around the strategic direction and the financial situation of the school, embraces the parent as a partner, and recognizes the Board's responsibility to communicate.

What does all of this mean? The answer is that you can't win the dollars conversation. Once the Board (and parents) start asking whether they can "afford" the school, that is a conversation it is almost impossible to win. However, when the conversation is around whether the school is delivering value to the student—providing an exceptional academic education, or a truly transformative faith-based experience, or an incredible character-growth experience, that is a conversation it is a delight to be a part of.

So tuition is about mission; parents' willingness to pay is based largely on their perception that they are receiving value. Schools with value will always be attractive to parents. So make your school the best it can be. That's your strategic task through your strategic plan. And that will enable your school to survive and thrive into the future.

Alternate Sources of Income

Boards wish to develop alternate sources of income so that the school becomes more "affordable." What might they be? Here are some ways to maximize the school's income.

- Ensure the Finance Committee really looks after the incoming monies well—interest on deposits can provide a nice supplement.
- Extended care programs (before and after school) provide both a valued service to the parent and an income stream for the school.

*ISM's publication, *The Tuition Book*, illustrates this chapter in greater detail. It is available at **isminc.com/bookstore**.

- ❖ Courses that are offered after school (including adult education) by school personnel offer faculty an opportunity to derive additional income and also provide revenue for the school.

- ❖ Summer programs introduce potential students and faculty to the school, utilize the facilities efficiently, create additional income opportunities for faculty, and can bring in revenue for the school.

- ❖ Endowment funds provide a steady revenue stream.

All of these are positive aspects of a school's overall programming, mission delivery, and income streams. None of them either individually or collectively will, for the vast majority of private-independent schools, ever be anything more than an adjunct to tuition. Tuition will remain the major source of income. So while you should support these endeavors as appropriate, you should also understand the centrality of tuition and never waver from its strategic importance.

Product, Process, Price

Consider one other very important reality in setting tuition. You compete in the marketplace (in a broad sense) on the basis of one of three stances:

- product,
- process, or
- price.

You must take responsibility for assisting your colleagues in working from a marketplace stance that fits your school's actual competitive platform.

Definitions

The product school. To generate the best product (defined here as seeking to be academically the premier school in your market, producing the best academically prepared students—what might be termed college prep).

The process school. To engage students in the best process (defined here as seeking to create a uniquely excellent physical and/or psychological learning environment). These schools might engage in uniquely excellent pedagogical approaches, provide the greatest array of student curricular and cocurricular choice, achieve the lowest possible student-staff and student-faculty ratios, and/or demonstrate other "process features" that set the school apart on the basis of the quality, quantity, and types of things it does every day.

The price school. To be different from those schools that strive to be "the best" by product or process measures. Schools in this category can compete on the basis of their marketable differences and, because their marketplace stance is so "different," on the basis of value and price. That is, they cost less than those schools in the first two categories because their priorities simply are not the same.

Which type of school—product, process, or price—is actually the best? The question has no meaning when worded in that way. The distinction is this: If a "difference/value/price" school attempts to take on the characteristics of a product- or process-based school, its planning emphasis and outcome may become badly distorted. As a result, the plan would be expensive in ways it should not be, given the context.

Implications of Your Marketplace Stance

Identify your marketplace stance using this three-category taxonomy. You can then carry that stance into, and through, your quadrennial strategic planning process.

The major ramifications are these.

- ❖ If your marketplace stance is "best product," you must accept the fact that your school will be expensive. You will, for example, invest heavily in next-level placement programs. For example, in a PK-12 school, you will have a college counseling program that reaches well down into the middle school. In a PK-8 school, you will have a high school preparation program. And you will put time and effort into gathering product-specific data regarding your graduates: both quality of placement and quality of performance.

- ❖ If your marketplace stance is "best process," you must accept the fact that your school will be even more expensive than "best product" schools. As implied in the earlier example, you will need the lowest possible student-staff and student-faculty ratios, a very expensive arrangement in itself. You will need the widest possible array of curricular and cocurricular offerings, both technology-based and not (e.g., extensive differentiation among levels of sports teams, numerous foreign language offerings, state-of-the-art-plus instructional technology, and continual attention to this aspect of teaching/learning).

You will invest perhaps less than the "product" school in staffing your next-level-placement counseling program, but much more in staffing your personal counseling program. You will invest in diversity—an expensive proposition unless your approach excludes, for example, socioeconomic considerations. And you will offer diversity-related programs to accompany your emphasis on the diverse make-up of your student body.

- If your marketplace stance is your "difference" (translated here as "best value" or "best price"), then you will need, in your strategic planning events, to guard assiduously against your planning colleagues' understandable eagerness to plan as if you were competing on the basis of product and/or process. Said another way, this means that in strategic planning your efforts should focus on being "more yourself," with all the not-necessarily-costly types of differences that that entails, and not "like" those schools in your area that compete on the basis of product and/or process. If you do seek to emulate them, you will inadvertently weaken your school's basic marketplace stance by making it **considerably more expensive, and *for the "wrong" kinds of reasons.***

The Marketplace Taxonomy: Overview

Schools can compete simultaneously on the basis of "product" and "process." Such schools become even more expensive than schools that compete on the basis of "just" product or "just" process. For example, such a PK-12 school would need both an extensive next-level-placement counseling staff and an extensive personal counseling staff, rather than emphasizing one over the other.

In contrast, schools cannot compete simultaneously on the basis of "difference" (defined here as including "value" or "price") on the one hand, and on the basis of "product" or "process" on the other. Difference/value/price-based schools can be relatively inexpensive and yet, at the same time, do a superb job of fulfilling their core reasons for existing. But they cannot effectively retain that marketplace stance and simultaneously seek to compete with product- or process-based marketplace competitors on their own turf.

Marketplace Stance and Tuition Implications

Take a look at the following table, which shows the kinds of dramatic differences in marketplace stance implied by the price/product/process choice. The hypothetical school depicted is PK-12 with enrollment of roughly 700. The table illustrates a *theoretical, ideal level* of staffing, pricing, facilities, and, in general, performance against the ISM Stability Markers.

Characteristic	Price	Product	Process
Student-faculty ratio	16:1	10:1	8:1
Student-staff ratio	11.7:1	5.8:1	5.1:1
Tuition (2008 $)	$7K	$20K	$25K
Faculty	44	70	88
Administrators/staff	16	50	50

Major Dangers

- Strategic planners (Board and senior administrators) in "difference/value/price" schools may seek to have "product/process" features without understanding the expense, and the probable loss of focus involved, as well, in shifting to a different marketplace stance. This creates a cost/value question in the marketplace.
- Strategic planners (Board and senior administrators) in "product" schools may seek "process" features without understanding the expense involved in moving to that marketplace stance.
- Strategic planners (Board and senior administrators) in "process" schools may continue to add such a plethora of programs and services that product (i.e., excellence of outcome) is eventually compromised through sheer overload and faculty/staff exhaustion.

So look at your mission, determine what your marketplace stance is, decide what you want your school to continue to be and/or to become, and then set tuition based on those considerations. The result will be a school that delivers what it promises (its mission), validates the decision of parents and students to attend, and is able to sustain excellence over time because it charges the tuition needed.

Base Tuition Gradient

The tuition gradient is an important number for you to know. It is the amount that tuition must increase in order for the school to keep what it has now at the same level of excellence. In other words, even if nothing changes, tuition will have to go up by the amount identified as the base tuition gradient.

How do you decide what your base tuition gradient should be to support the strategic financial plan? Clearly, this number is intended to cover inflationary costs so that the value of the fees your school receives does not erode over time. However, the Consumer Price Index-Urban (CPI-U) does not completely reflect expenditures in private-independent schools; it can only serve as a base figure. The base tuition gradient for private-independent schools is inflation (adjusted for your local area) plus 2%. If you're happy with this explanation, you can skip the next, more technical, paragraphs and go on to the next chapter.

Technical Explanations

The following is provided for you (given the importance of the base tuition gradient concept for tuition setting) in case you really distrust this idea, or just want to understand it better.

The CPI has a built-in "productivity factor." It assumes that the work force is increasingly productive as computers, streamlined mechanical devices, and other labor-saving developments provide greater output with fewer personnel. The more efficient business becomes, the more inflation is stabilized or reduced.

Education differs from those kinds of industries in that it is people-intensive and not product-driven. Education cannot offset the total true effects of inflation by increased efficiency—the classroom still consists of a teacher and a group of students. If more students enroll, we create more sections with more teachers. Furthermore, even as the demand for additional programs (and teachers) occurs, schools tend not to remove any of the existing programs to lessen the budgetary crunch. Costs go up even when productivity remains static.

Baumol's Cost Disease. All service industries suffer from a phenomenon commonly called Baumol's cost disease.* William Baumol, renowned economist at New York University, developed data that indicated costs in service-related businesses inherently rise faster than in product-oriented industries. This occurs because productivity in the labor-intensive service sector tends to lag behind manufacturing, and salaries in the service sector have to keep up with salaries in more productive industries. In short, the costs for health care, entertainment, insurance, law enforcement, and education will always rise faster than overall inflation.

More recently, economists Jack E. Triplett and Barry P. Bosworth reaffirmed Baumol's findings and inferences concerning productivity. They claim the problem comes in the "mismeasurement of output." How do you measure the productivity of a teacher, and thus quantify the salary cost? For tech-savvy teachers, computers can possibly improve productivity in the classroom. But labor-intensive industries (like education) have a limited ability to benefit from technological advances and inevitably experience higher real costs. The CPI can reflect the costs of producing automobiles or computers, but it is clearly a poor base for setting tuitions (which are largely determined by faculty compensation, your school's primary budget item).

Private-independent schools must compete with other industries when attracting and retaining qualified employees—they must pay market-competitive salaries to maintain a mission-appropriate, skilled staff. If faculty compensation must rise at a greater rate than inflation, so must tuition.

The 2%+ Factor and Your Tuition. To increase productivity, each teacher would have to teach larger classes (unpopular with parents, students, and teachers) or teach more classes (unpopular with overworked faculty who may seek other employment if the load is too high). To maintain an equivalent operation, year to year, you need income that is at least 2% greater than the CPI to cover the additional hidden inflation. If your school does not keep one step ahead financially, quality will eventually be eroded through decreased faculty morale, diminished services, and deferred maintenance.

---

*Baumol's "diagnosis" first appeared in his 1967 paper, *Macroeconomics of Unbalanced Growth: The Anatomy of Urban Crisis, American Economic Review* 57(3), pp. 415-426. For a detailed explanation of Baumol's cost disease, see "What Ails Us," from the Financial Page of *The New Yorker* (July 7, 2003). See also "Productivity in the Services Sector," *Brookings Economic Papers*, January 2000. The full PDF version is available online at **www.brook.edu/views/papers/triplett/20000112.htm**. There is also evidence that private schools suffer more from Baumol's disease than public schools, primarily due to reduced class size. See "Trends in Private School Cost and Tuition: No Immunity From the Cost Disease," a paper given at the 1998 AEFA Meeting by F. Howard Nelson, Senior Associate Director of the Department of Research, American Federation of Teachers. More information concerning the Consumer Price Index can be found at **www.bls.gov/cpi**. If you would like an index that reflects the cost of living for your immediate geographic area, your regional office of the Bureau of Labor Statistics can supply you with local CPI listings.

Faculty Culture

Guiding Principle: Board-level strategic support of a healthy, growth-oriented faculty culture is critical for the school to sustain long-term programmatic excellence.

The faculty are the intersect of the mission with the students. The performance of all students (as an entire group) is dependent on the way in which teachers (all of them) carry out their responsibilities. This "way" is the faculty culture: the pattern of customs, ideas, and assumptions driving the faculty's collective set of professional attitudes and behaviors. The outcome of a healthy faculty culture is sustained/enhanced student performance, enthusiasm, and satisfaction.

The faculty are, however, an operational responsibility and you, as a Trustee, should not interfere in their daily work. So what are the strategic ways in which you can aid the Management Team in ensuring a healthy culture? Going back to the ISM X, the question can be reframed: What resources can you as a Trustee provide that Executive Leadership (the Management Team) can translate into the interpersonal variables at the top of X? There are four.

1. Require the School Head to develop (or sustain) an **evaluation system** for faculty that is predicated on each faculty member's commitment to her/his own professional growth and career. This is ISM's researched correlate to student performance, enthusiasm, and satisfaction. This commitment is the measurement point for predicting a school's academic success and its ability to retain (and also recruit) its students. In this system, evaluation is a synonym for professional development that guides each teacher's professional growth and, by implication, capacity building.

2. Support this professional development by moving (or sustaining) the professional development line of the **budget** toward/at 2% of operational expenses. This is the simplest investment that you as a Trustee can make and provides the biggest return on that investment. This budget line should be defended in times of scarcity, and defended over cuts in either personnel or program. It's that important.
3. Ensure that you have and support **competitive faculty salaries**, i.e., salaries that are within 95% of your target group, whether it is your group/ association of private-independent schools, or the local public school system, or a group of schools with the same philosophy as yours. Through the quadrennial strategic planning process, as well as in the annual budget setting that the strategic planning drives, demonstrate to your faculty that they are valued and will, from a Board/resource point of view, be well cared for.
4. Ensure that your school has and supports **extensive employee benefits**. Research on retention and recruitment shows that the compensation package the school offers (Board isn't the employer) has a significant impact on its ability to hire and keep excellent employees.

Your actions in supporting these four faculty initiatives provide a resource framework for the Management Team. This framework allows the team to work successfully in developing and sustaining a faculty culture that supports your school's:

- competitive advantage;
- ability to attract mission-appropriate students, now and in the future; and
- ability to attract exemplary faculty who can deliver the mission at a standard of excellence to those students.

CD-ROM References

"RSM Study: Final Outcomes," *I&P* 25.9
"Faculty Evaluation, Student Performance, and School Leadership: An Update," *I&P* 31.13
"Pizza, Compensation, and Faculty Culture: Is It Time for Merit Pay?" *I&P* 30.5
"A Practical Approach to Broadbanding," *I&P* 30.9
"Employee Benefits for Faculty: Examine Your School's Contribution to Health Insurance," *I&P*, 30.12

Development

Guiding Principle:

1. *Development is not (or should not be) critical to day-to-day operations. Development IS critical for enabling the school to take significant steps into the future and for enhancing the education of the students.*
2. *Development is not fund raising. It is the process by which schools identify, cultivate, solicit, recognize and steward their donors/prospects to establish and nurture relationships and raise resources.*

Definitions

- **Philanthropy** occurs when individuals give according to their values and interests.
- **Development** is about uncovering individuals' values and interests through the identification, cultivation, solicitation, recognition, and stewardship of donors and prospects.
- **Fund raising**, which resides within solicitation, allows individuals to act upon their values and interests through their giving.
- **Donor-centered, values-based fund raising** is based on this understanding of *philanthropy, development, and fund raising.*

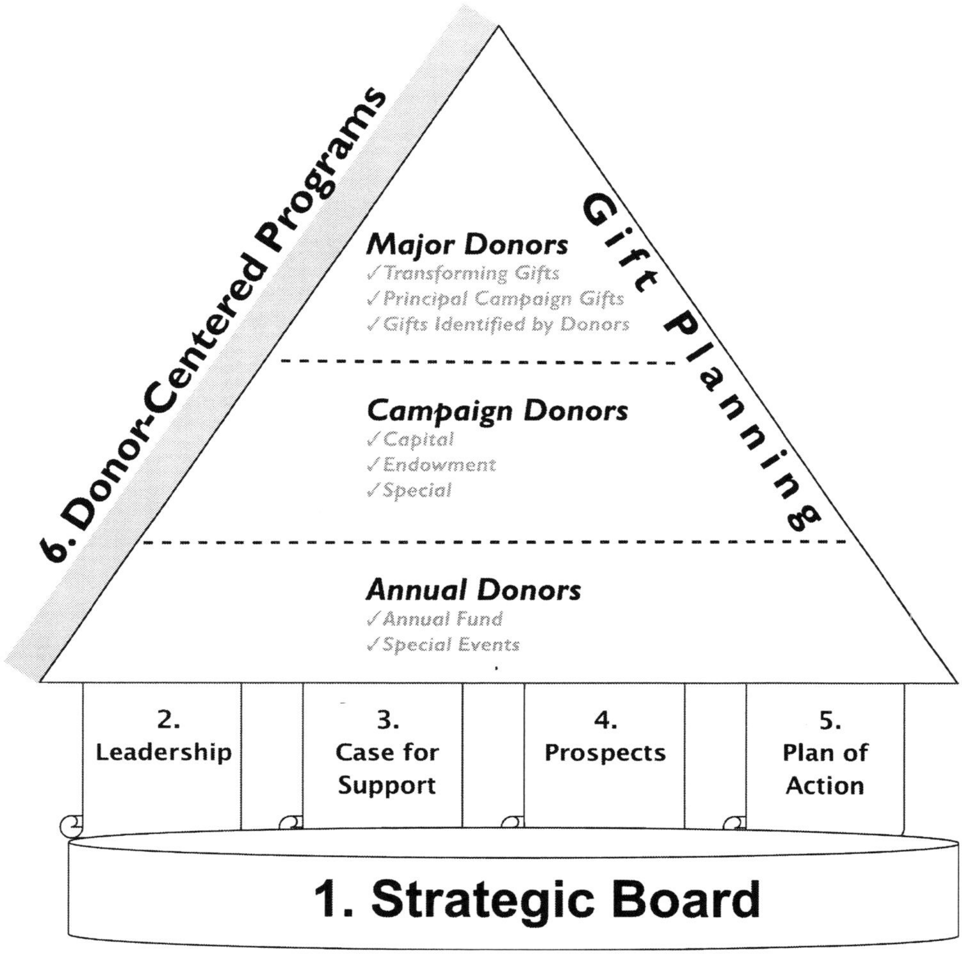

The Comprehensive Development Model

In looking at the Comprehensive Development Model, note the following points.

❖ Development will not reach its potential without the solid foundation of strategic planning. When the Board acts with the long-term good of the school in mind and understands the importance of thinking in a way that benefits generations, not just individuals. That provides the development effort with the means to generate confidence in the future of the school among its most loyal supporters, as well as for those whose connection is much weaker.

- As a Trustee, you are automatically part of the leadership bench strength of the school. You set the tone and pace to inspire and motivate other volunteers to ask and donors to give. You help establish the climate within which a culture of philanthropy can grow and thrive. You will be a part of the Annual Giving campaign each year as a donor and in some leadership capacity, and you will attend development special events to show support through your presence and your generosity. The level at which you give should represent the fact that your school is either first or second on your list of philanthropic gifts.

  Note: The annual fund is the foundation of all fund-raising efforts. By creating a culture of giving at your school, it connects to the broadest possible group of donors, instilling a habit of giving. The annual fund provides the base from which donors "bubble up" to your other, larger fund-raising efforts, especially and including your major gift program.

- The idea of identifying prospects is not coming up with a long list of people whose arms you are employed to twist! Rather, it is the acknowledgment that there are those whose relationship with the school is valued and nurtured and who, when the moment comes, give because of their increasing interest in the school. More importantly, they will continue to give because you maintain that relationship and steward that person now not just as your friend, but as the school's friend.

The Role of the Board of Trustees

The development process is directed by the development leadership, which includes the Board President, the School Head, the Chair of the Development Committee, and the Development Director.

As an enthusiastic Board member who has a clear picture of your school's students, faculty, mission, priorities, and funding needs, you will assume the following duties.

- You contribute to the fullest measure within your means to annual, capital, and endowment campaigns, and the major gift program.

- You set the standard of giving for others with your own contribution.

  Donors and prospects look to the Board for leadership when considering their own gifts. The philanthropic commitment of your Board helps to create the culture of philanthropy in your school and leads fund-raising efforts for your internal and external constituencies.

- ❖ You are involved in identifying, cultivating, soliciting, recognizing, and stewarding major gift prospects/donors. (See "The Donor Cultivation Cycle" in this chapter.) Examples of effective involvement might include:
  - continually identifying individuals to bring them closer to your school;
  - annually cultivating and stewarding a portfolio of donors, e.g., calling and updating donors who have already given on what is happening at the school, reminding them that their gift made a difference, and inviting them to those programs and activities that match their values and interests;
  - introducing donors to other solicitation team members during visits;
  - writing follow-up and acknowledgment letters; and
  - hosting small gatherings.
- ❖ You serve in leadership roles, which may include becoming a:
  - Chair of the Annual Fund Cabinet or a Chair of one of its divisions (Leadership, Parents, Alumni, Faculty, or Staff),
  - Chair or member of the Development Committee,
  - Chair or member of the Major Gift Committee, or
  - solicitation team member, either as solicitor, educator, or cultivator.
- ❖ You also act as the public face of the school providing testimony, including, for example:
  - being featured in your school's annual report or magazine, and
  - hosting parlor meetings or dinner dialogues.

The Donor-Centered Approach to Development

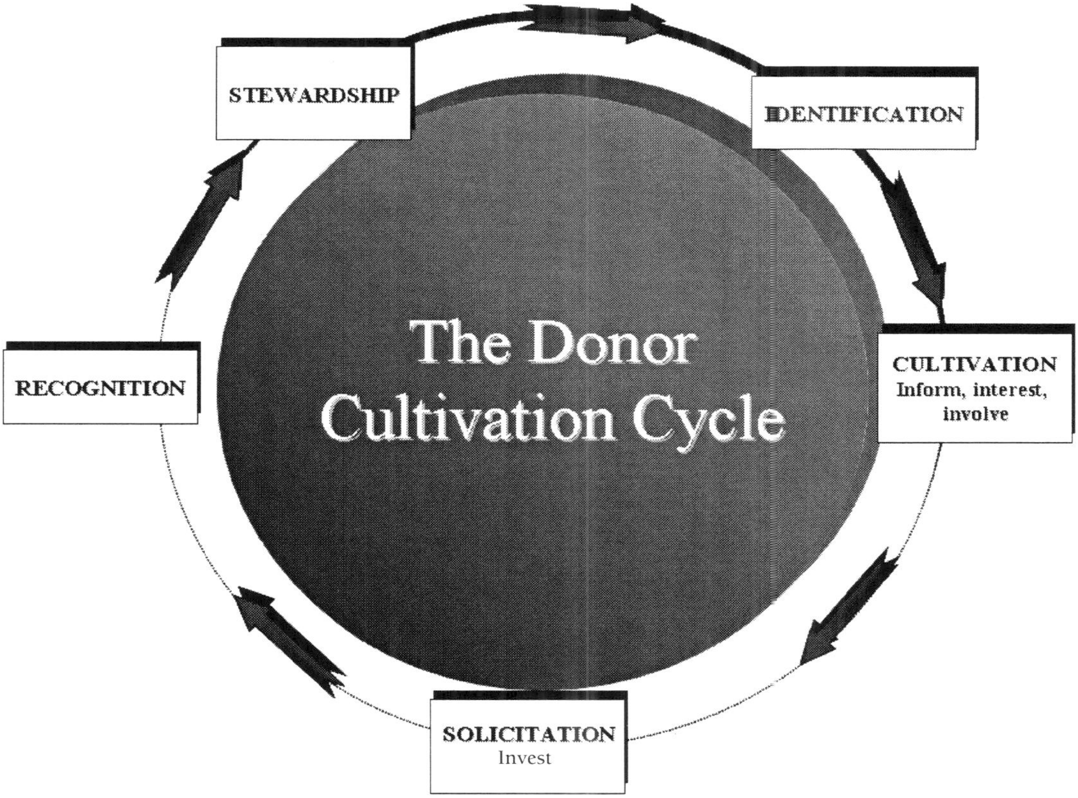

The Development Committee

While every Trustee should be involved in some aspect of development, the work of the Board is organized through its Development Committee. The individual(s) who chair(s) the Development Committee, in partnership with the Board President, School Head, and Development Director, is responsible for the planning, development, and implementation of a comprehensive development program aligned with the school's strategic and long-range plans.

The core tasks of the Development Committee are:

- to create a strategic development plan,
- to recruit people who will take responsibility for specific tasks in the plan, and

- to encourage other Trustees and non-members to give and to help get financial support.

These tasks are incorporated in the Board of Trustees' charge to its Development Committee.

Major Gift Committee

A major gift program is part of an effective development effort, and is distinct from annual giving. The Major Gift Committee is a subcommittee of the Development Committee.

The purpose of this committee is to identify, cultivate, solicit, recognize, and steward the very top donors whose gifts can and will make a difference to the long-term future of your school. This program should be initiated through the identification of 10 or more individuals whose capacity and demonstrated interest in the school would make them prospects to give a significant gift in some future campaign. This effort is not staff driven. It lies solely within the province of the Board and is essential to the eventual success of a large capital campaign.

CD-ROM References

"18 Characteristics of a Major Gifts Program," *I&P* 21.9
"A Comprehensive Development Model," *I&P* 30.4
"Development Office Management: The ISM Stability Marker," *I&P* 32.4
"The Buck Starts Here: Philanthropic Responsibilities of Your Board," *I&P* 32.3
"The Development Quartet: The Core Leadership Team of the Comprehensive Development Model," *I&P* 31.16
"The Annual Fund Cabinet: A Volunteer-Professional Partnership," *TTP* 10.6
"The Donor Cultivation Cycle and Your Annual Fund," *TTP* 13.6

Head Support and Evaluation Committee

Guiding Principle: *The Board's only employee is the School Head; support of the School Head is of paramount importance so that, in evaluation of the School Head, there is every hope for success, predictability in the process, and a complete absence of surprises for either side.*

There is a strange paradox in the process of supporting and evaluating the School Head. Yes, the School Head is the Board's only employee. That means the Board must hold her/him accountable. But the Board is incapable of doing that! Remember that you are a volunteer with limited time. Think of everything the Head is responsible for overseeing:

- the entire academic program
- the entire athletic program
- the cocurricular program
- human resources
- facilities
- re-recruitment and recruitment of students
- marketing of the school
- parent relations

- development
- evaluation
- legal matters
- health and safety issues
- scheduling
- janitorial services
- food services ... and the list goes on

The point here is that it's just not possible for the Board with its competencies to oversee the position of School Head effectively. Furthermore, the job is so enormous that if you tried to evaluate on the exceptional fulfillment of all these tasks, chances are that most Heads would fail! So the questions "Who evaluates?" and "What do they evaluate?" are very important ones. You are responsible for answering them!

The best practice is to delegate this task to a special committee of the Board called the Head Support and Evaluation Committee. It serves an advice and counsel function (i.e., no contract or compensation function) that resides within the Executive Committee. You may be invited to be a part of this committee but should only accept if you meet quite specific criteria.

- ❖ You have significant CEO-like leadership experience (e.g., in a small business, a large United Way campaign, a symphony Board, or a division of a medium-sized corporation).
- ❖ You are a strategic thinker, demonstrating that in your contributions to committee and Board work.
- ❖ You have a reputation for supportive, positively reinforcing behaviors.
- ❖ You have absolutely no special or private agendas of your own.
- ❖ You are neither hostile to, nor a sycophant of, the School Head.

Selection of the committee members is all-important. The HSEC is chaired by a Board member. However, the rest of the slots can be filled by those best qualified to fill the role, Board or non-Board. Often, for example, the current or former Head of a non-competing private school serves as a non-Board member of the HSEC. Note that the "support" function is so critical that the Head should be given an informal veto power over the selection of members on the committee. (However, if abused, this courtesy will be withdrawn.)

The following sequence of steps outlines the process.

1. The Executive Committee reviews the strategic plan annually and writes the annual agenda.
2. The School Head writes the annual administration agenda, drawing from:
   - the annual agenda,
   - unfinished planning document items from the previous year(s), and
   - any other major operational initiatives.
3. The Executive Committee creates, renews, or reconstitutes your Head Support and Evaluation Committee, and supplies its Chair with her/his charge. As with all Board committees, the HSEC should receive its formal charge annually and in writing.
4. The HSEC members, together with the School Head, agree on the five or so objectives drawn from the annual administration agenda (and, rarely, aspects of your Head's performance that need to be addressed) on which the Head will be evaluated. These objectives are not due diligence items—matters that the Head is expected to fulfill as part of normal job requirements. They are objectives that will make a difference in the life of the school.
5. The HSEC then reflects with the Head on her/his commitment to the school mission, particularly as it relates to the Head's own personal/professional objectives. Ask the Head to consider strengths and weaknesses that should inform the coming year's objectives and derive a professional development objective from those. Add that to the five objectives. The HSEC establishes data points that will denote progress/completion/success for each of those objectives (including the professional development objective). Finally, it creates a time line that shows when the Head and the HSEC will meet in order to talk about progress, seek support, and move to success.
6. This document is then presented to the Board for information (not approval, given that the Board has already approved the strategic plan). Some Boards and Heads choose, in addition, to publish these objectives in the school newsletter. This is a good idea. It makes sense to educate your constituents about the Board's/Head's direction for the year both in terms of gaining support for them and in managing expectations around directions that are not being taken.

7. The HSEC then continues to monitor the process on a regular basis throughout the year. The HSEC Committee reports to the Executive Committee.
8. The Executive Committee acts on the report to establish a basis for annual compensation reviews with the School Head and to recommend to the Board both a compensation package as well as a continuation of the Head's two-year rolling contract (where merited).

What's the alternative to this process? Boards very typically do the following:

- carry out some form of 360-degree survey where people's opinions of the Head are solicited (Note: 360-degree surveys are NEVER to be used for evaluative purposes, for the Head or anyone else in the organization—only for professional development purposes),
- hand out a form at a Board meeting at some point in the spring for Trustees to complete, and
- have a discussion based on the information gleaned from the surveys and the filled-in forms.

The weaknesses of this alternative approach are many. Evaluation conducted this way:

- tends to be related to the school's strategic plan only incidentally, if at all, and thus is not constructed around the Head's basic "job description"—fulfilling the school's planning document;
- tends to use criteria that are unwritten, unspoken, and, typically, known only after the fact (by the Head and perhaps by most of the Trustees);
- tends to rely for the most critical judgments upon the Trustees themselves, regardless of whether the Trustees have been engaged with the Head and/or with the school in ways likely to produce informed judgments;
- tends to rest, in whole or in part, upon a checklist or a rating form that is used repeatedly, from year to year, despite the evolutionary nature of the school's, and consequently the Head's, performance requirements;
- tends toward judgment only: that is, it seldom displays characteristics that could be termed "developmental" (which, being developmental, would foster improvement in Head and school performance during the school year); and
- tends to be mostly subjective and impressionistic—measurable objectives and data relevant to those objectives are seldom incorporated into the process.

Remember that support and evaluation of the Head is one of the Board's most important roles. It must be done effectively, respectfully, and supportively. Doing it well furthers the institution's goals and cements a proactive relationship.

CD-ROM References

"Board/Head Relationships: Brutal Facts and Eternal Faith," *I&P* 28.16
"Is Your School's Head Evaluation Just a 'Form'ality?" *TTP* 7.4
"Head Evaluation: 10 Steps to an Approach That Gets Results," *TTP* 10.8
"Caveats for the Head Evaluation Committee," *I&P* 21.15
"Xcellence in Executive Leadership: A School Head Evaluation Instrument (Part One)," *I&P* 30.5
"Xcellence in Executive Leadership: A School Head Evaluation Instrument (Part Two)," *I&P* 30.6
"The Head Support and Evaluation Committee: What Does 'Support' Actually Mean?" *I&P* 30.7
"Questions the Head Candidate Should Ask Concerning the School's Planning Document," *I&P* 25.10
"Financial Questions the Head Candidate Should Ask During the Interviews," *I&P* 26.13
"Board Support for the Head's Difficult Personnel Decisions," *TTP* 13.6
"Avoiding Unnecessary Head Changes," *I&P* 22.8
"The Board's Contract With the School Head: Solidify Expectations, Define Relationships," *I&P*, 32.1

Other Board-Level Committees

> ***Guiding Principle:*** *Board committees exist to serve specific needs of the strategic plan. All committees are thus ad hoc. Five committees "look" permanent because they always have a strategic function, e.g., Executive, Finance, Development, Trustees, and Head Support and Evaluation.*

Note: The job of all committees is a subset of the strategic plan. Each committee is charged with carrying out a particular group of objectives that are directly (and by implication) derived from the annual agenda. As the figure on page 75 illustrates, the strategic plan drives the Board's annual agenda; this determines what the Board needs to accomplish in any given year. Those objectives identify the Board's calendar for the year and determine the committees needed to bring about success. This is the reason Board committees are "ad hoc" in principle—they exist in order to fulfill strategic plan objectives. *Committees should not exist when they have no strategic function.*

The Executive Committee

The first job of this committee is not complicated.

1. Create the annual agenda using the appropriate year of the strategic plan to identify the items that the Board is responsible for.
2. Identify the Committees necessary to carry out those items and write charges for them.
3. Create the Board meeting timetable, identifying appropriate times to meet based on the reporting time line of the committees. Each meeting is

determined by the need for the Board to take action based on the report and recommendation of each committee.

4. Execute the annual retreat in June/July (scheduling time for everyone to note the dates of meetings for the year and set aside that time).
5. Carry out a mid-year review of the agenda.
6. Support the Committee on Trustees in its work with individual Trustees (both commending and counseling out).

The second task involves the Head's contract. Each year, the Head Support and Evaluation Committee will report on the Head's performance to the Executive Committee and recommend continuation or termination of the contract. It is the Executive Committee's function to renew the Head's contract, negotiating with the Head as to the terms, and to take that contract to the Board for approval. Alternatively, it may be time to ask the Board not to renew and, instead, to instigate the Head search process.

Outside of extraordinary circumstances as outlined in the Board bylaws, these are the two tasks of this committee. Typically, this committee is composed of Board officers.

Finance Committee

While there may be specific charges because of the annual agenda for that year, there are also some ongoing tasks that the Finance Committee carries out:

- creation or maintenance of the strategic financial plan,
- preparation with the School Head and Business Manager of the budget for recommendation to the Board,
- development and implementation of Business Office policies,
- review of the school's finances on a monthly basis,
- review of the school's annual audit, and
- aid in the preparation of the annual report.

Typically, there will be four to six members of this committee (in addition to the Business Manager), most of whom are Trustees. These individuals understand organizational finance and want to understand how that applies to private-independent schools.

Committee on Trustees

In many ways this is the most important committee in terms of sustaining the Board's ability to be excellent over a long period of time. Its prime responsibility is Trustee performance, which carries this out through three processes in the life of a Trustee.

1. **Trustee profiling**. By looking at the strategic plan, the committee can determine the needs of the Board at least three years into the future and thus identify the kind of person who would best be able to advance the school. Prospective members are profiled for the wealth, work, and wisdom needed to effectively staff the Board and carry out the strategic plan objectives. You are reading this because you have one or more characteristics that are valuable in moving the school forward.
2. **Trustee education**. This committee creates the education process for the Board, from ensuring that new Trustees are given all the materials they need, to organizing the Board retreat, to providing the new Trustee with a Board mentor, to checking in with the committees to see what support they need to be effective.
3. **Trustee accountability**. Every year, this committee conducts the Board evaluation and receives feedback and observations about individual Trustee performance. This enables it to identify Trustees who are either not mission appropriate, not pulling their weight, or acting in ways that do not strengthen the Board team. The committee then has the task of counseling out the Trustee.

While all Trustees have much to do, this committee is a year-round undertaking. If you are asked to be a member of this committee (composed exclusively of Trustees), this will likely be the only Committee you can serve on.

CD-ROM References

"Planning Overview: The Long Range and Strategic Approaches," *TTP* 5.8
"Strategic Bylaws: Unleash your Board Committees," *TTP* 12.7
"Today's Executive Committee," *TTP* 11.7
"The Role of the Finance Committee," *TTP* 11.5
"The Development Committee Calendar," *I&P* 22.3
"Charging Board Committees: A Recommended Format," *I&P* 28.9

The Trustee's Commitment to Growth

Guiding Principle: *Trustees must commit to growth and renewal so that they are able to contribute at a more and more sophisticated level to the needs of the school.*

If you come from the corporate sector, 20% of what you know is irrelevant to private-independent schools, 60% is very useful in being a Trustee, and 20% will actually destroy the school. It is thus important to "know your school," and also to "know your industry." Trustees therefore agree to learn and become competent, if not expert, in what they do.

There are three basic ways you develop as a Trustee.

1. **Participate fully in the orientation process.**

   - Study the Board policy manual and other relevant documents such as the strategic plan/strategic financial plan and Board bylaws.
   - At the annual Board retreat, make sure you clearly understand the presentations on Board governance, committee responsibilities, and the initiatives the school is undertaking.
   - Gain a clear understanding of what the Committee or Trustees expects of you.

2. **Learn as you go.**

    - Read the supporting materials sent with each Board agenda so you can participate intelligently and concisely in the discussions at the meetings.
    - Many Boards set up a mentoring process, matching each new member with an experienced Trustee. Ask your mentor all those "stupid" questions!

3. **Take responsibility for expanding your knowledge.**

    - Attend at least two major events during the school year so that you understand, at a student level, why this school is so exciting. Of course, if you are a parent, you will be there a lot more!
    - Read articles pertaining to your position as a Trustee and/or to your committee responsibilities, e.g., ISM's *Ideas & Perspectives* and *To The Point* advisory publications.
    - Read your school's Web site at least once a year.

These actions support you in being a proactive and effective leader in the school's governance.

Board Meetings

The content of Board meetings is a direct outcome of strategic planning. This is how it works:

Strategic planning
A three-day process with the Head and Board

↓

Annual agenda
Items to be dealt with as outlined in that year's strategic plan

↓ ↓

Board agenda **Annual administration agenda**
Set by the Executive Committee each spring

↓

Committees and their charges
Written by the Executive Committee as a result of examining the needs identified in the Board agenda

↓

Board calendar
Established after the Executive Committee has determined with each Chair when that committee's particular charges will be ready for Board action, e.g.:

- Budget by November;
- Development plan by September;
- Master facilities plan by February;
- Head support and evaluation by April;
- Board profile by April

Meeting agendas. Each agenda is set with the central piece of the meeting being the committee's recommendation for action (no more than two action items and usually only one per meeting).

The meeting agenda is predictable, accountable, and puts the accent on action.

Two-hour meeting (example)

10 minutes for administrative business

90 minutes to discuss and decide the main strategic item(s) of the meeting based on a Board committee's recommendation for action

10 minutes for next steps

5 minutes for celebration (of either Board or school accomplishments)

5 minutes for reflection (what went well/poorly in the meeting)

CD-ROM References

"Planning Overview: The Long Range and Strategic Approaches," *TTP* 5.8
"The Long and Short of Board Minutes," *TTP* 11.6

Change

> ***Guiding Principle:*** *Change happens well in private-independent schools when it is mission-based, student-centered, provided with necessary resources, founded on strategic planning, supported by excellent school leadership, and carried out with perseverance.*

Boards, being proactive and typically ambitious for their schools, are often agents of change. Be aware that change for its own sake, or to please a particular constituency or person, or without regard to the complexity of schools is more destructive than productive. So as a Trustee, consider the following.

- ❖ Concentrate your efforts on the very small number of productive possibilities that will make the biggest difference—these can be tested through the lenses of the school's mission and the ISM Stability Markers.
- ❖ Faculty are not resistant to change—they are inundated by it. What they want is change that is:
  - connected to mission and, by implication, the lives of students;
  - well-resourced, i.e., supported with money and time and materials;
  - carried out with administrative perseverance: If "I" put effort into this, you won't change your mind a year from now.

- ❖ Recognize that any significant change you want will cost money, and usually imply an increase in tuition to pay for it. If you don't want to raise tuition, don't try the change.
- ❖ Let the strategic plan determine the timing and the pace of any change event, whether it be a construction project, a new marketing plan, an additional position, or an extended budget for professional development.
- ❖ Understand that, in change, matters get worse before they get better. (See the "Implementation Dip" illustration below.) Don't expect immediate improvement—you must be patient.

At the same time, don't be afraid of change, especially on the basis that "it didn't work last time." Go through a reflective process to think about why the last effort was not successful and determine to learn from that experience. Your school must move forward, and the face of education changes rapidly.

To stay competitive, you must continue to serve your students and their parents. Always work strategically with a sense of moral purpose. Always plan carefully from a mission-based understanding of the advantages that will accrue. Always resource the improvement so that it can be sustained. Support the School Head through the implementation dip when people may become impatient. You will be successful and your school will thrive.

Illustration of the Implementation Dip

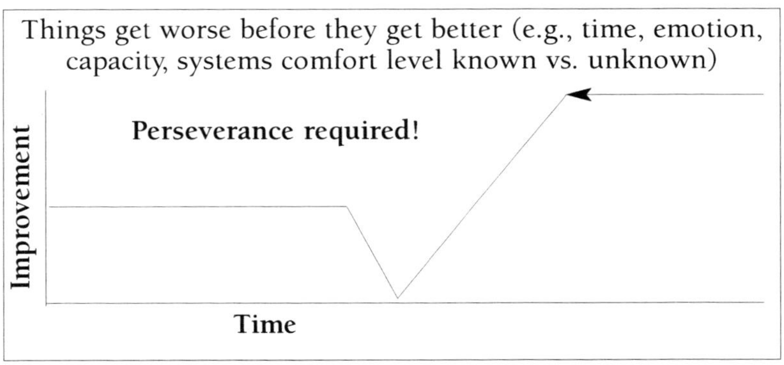

CD-ROM References

"Mission and Leadership: A Primer in Mission-Oriented 'Change' Problems," *I&P* 29.8
"Reculturing for Change: A Head's Primer/Change and the Implementation Dip," *I&P* 29.1
"Managing Complex Change in Private-Independent Schools," *I&P* 30.4

Appendix 1: Sample Committee Charge Sheet

School Year: ____

Board Committee: ____

Board Committee Chair: ____

Reference Documents: ____

Committee Charge(s):

1. ____

____

____

____

Specific Reference: ____

Date due (Board meeting): ____

2. ____

____

____

____

Specific Reference: ____

Date due (Board meeting): ____

Other responsibilities: ____

____

____

____

Appendix 2: Samples of Conflict-of-Interest Policies

Sample 1

The Board shall not enter into any contract or transaction with (a) one or more of its Trustees, (b) a director of a related organization, or (c) an organization in or of which a Trustee of [school name] is a Director, officer, or legal representative, or in some other way has a material financial interest unless:

- that interest is disclosed or known to the Board of Trustees;
- the Board approves, authorizes, or ratifies the action in good faith;
- the approval is by a majority of Trustees (not counting the interested Trustee); and
- it is approved at a meeting where a quorum is present (not counting the interested Trustee).

The interested Trustee may not be present for discussion to answer questions, may not advocate for the action to be taken, and must leave the room while a vote is taken. The minutes of all actions taken on such matters shall clearly reflect that these requirements have been met.

Sample 2

The Charities Review Council of Minnesota recommends that nonprofit Boards have Directors sign an annual statement regarding conflicts. One potential statement is as follows:

The undersigned person acknowledges receipt of a copy of the [school name] Board of Trustees' "Resolution Concerning Conflict of Interest" dated ___/___/___. By my signature affixed below, I acknowledge my agreement with the spirit and intent of this resolution and I agree to report to the President of the Board of Trustees any possible conflicts (other than those stated below) that may develop before completion of the next annual statement.

_______ I am not aware of any conflict of interest

_______ I have a conflict of interest in the following area(s)

(Adapted from "Management Assistance Program for Nonprofits," 2233 University Avenue West, #360, Saint Paul, MN 55114)

Sample 3

Many organizations adopt a conflict-of-interest policy. Carver Governance Design, Inc. (2060 Kingdom Drive, Columbus, IN 47201) suggests the following Directors' Code of Conduct, which includes information regarding conflict of interest.

Directors' Code of Conduct

The Board expects of itself and its members ethical and businesslike conduct. This commitment includes proper use of authority and appropriate decorum in group and individual behavior when acting as directors.

1. Directors must represent unconflicted loyalty to the interests of the ownership.
    - This accountability supersedes any conflicting loyalty such as that to advocacy or interest groups and membership on other Boards or staffs.
    - This accountability supersedes the personal interest of any Director acting as an individual consumer of this agency's services.
2. Directors must avoid any conflict of interest with respect to their fiduciary responsibility.
    - There must be no self-dealing or any conduct of private business or personal services between any Director and the agency except as procedurally controlled to assure openness, competitive opportunity, and equal access to otherwise "inside" information.
    - Directors must not use their positions to obtain for themselves or for their family members employment within the agency.
    - Should a Director be considered for employment, he/she must temporarily withdraw from Board deliberation, voting, and access to applicable Board information.
3. Directors may not attempt to exercise individual authority over the agency except as explicitly set forth in Board policies.

- Directors' interaction with the Executive Director or with staff must recognize the lack of authority in any individual Director or group of Directors except as noted above.
- Directors' interaction with the public, press, or other entities must recognize the same limitation and the similar inability of any Director or Directors to speak for the Board.
- Directors will make no judgments of the Executive Director or staff performance except as that performance is assessed against explicit Board policies by the official process.

4. Directors will deal with outside entities or individuals, with clients and staff, and with each other in a manner reflecting fair play, ethics, and straightforward communication.

Appendix 3: Sample Board and Committee Calendar

The sample calendar on these two pages is descriptive, not prescriptive, and is not intended to be exhaustive.

Month	Board	Executive	Finance	Head Support and Evaluation	Development	Committee on Trustees
April	Meeting; Board self-evaluation	Review/revise the strategic plan and strategic financial plan	Review tuition fee schedule as necessary from the SFP		Review progress of annual fund campaign: set goal for next year; review SFP and identify objectives for coming year	Counsel out ineffective Trustees; prepare for summer retreat; effect the self-evaluation process by the Board
May	Meeting	Determine committee charges, choose Chairs for them and work with those Chairs on membership	Review monthly reports from the Business Office	Develop annual objectives for the Head	Select Chairs for coming campaign/s; plan materials for Development Office to produce over summer	Nomination of new Trustees
June	Annual Retreat; Approve agenda for the year	Set the Board agenda for the coming year; carry out the annual retreat; carry out process for Head's contract renewal as required	Review monthly reports from the Business Office	Provide report regarding Head's carrying out of previous year's objectives to Executive Committee	Confirm Development Committee members for the coming year	Annual Board evaluation; recommendations for any changes in structure; lead retreat

Month	Board	Executive	Finance	Head Support and Evaluation	Development	Committee on Trustees
July/ August			Study and approve the school's annual audit		Review and identify leadership gifts	New Trustee orientation
September	Meetings begin with strategic focus	Monitor Committees' progress; hold Board to strategic meetings	Review Business Office procedures; prepare summary reports for the school	Monitor and support Head in carrying out objectives	Board/faculty solicitation complete; annual campaign kickoff	
October	Meeting		Review monthly reports from the Business Office	Meeting	Phonathon and personal solicitation	Cultivation of profiled Board prospects
November	Meeting		First draft budget presented	Meeting	Begin review of enhancements for next year's campaign	Aid Executive Committee to ensure effectiveness of whole Board meetings
December	Meeting: budget approval		Budget presented to Board		Conclude Annual Campaign	Follow-up orientation
January	Semi-annual retreat	Mid-year review of agendas	Review monthly reports from the Business Office	Semi-annual retreat	Review	
February		Prepare plans to repeat the process	Review monthly reports from the Business Office	Meeting		
March	Meeting		Review monthly reports from the Business Office	Meeting	Repeat the process	Update Board profile based on strategic plan

Appendix 4: Sample Strategic Board Bylaws

While there is no "standard" approach to the formulation of private-independent school bylaws, Boards should periodically review these items to:

1. make them clearer, simpler, and more utilitarian; and
2. bring them more fully into the day-to-day life of the Board and of the school.

Boards exist to ensure that the institution's mission will be viable for the current students' children. Because the primary constituency the Board is charged with serving does not yet exist, an orientation toward the future is implicit. Thus, it follows that any Board's core activity is strategic planning—i.e., creating and overseeing the implementation of a viability-focused institutional road map.

Implications for Bylaws

Consider revisiting your Board's bylaws to determine the extent to which they reflect and promote that core planning activity. If they do, or if your Board's leadership is willing to edit or rewrite them so that they will, then your bylaws can become an integral component in your Board's actual structure and function. The following outline may be helpful as you review your bylaws to ascertain the extent to which they are "strategic." Recommended ingredients in such an approach would include the following.

- **An approval (cover) sheet**. A cover sheet showing your bylaws' date of approval, with appropriate signature(s), and with ratifications, if any, from other authorities (e.g., a parent religious body) provides an appropriate introductory page.

- **A philosophical source sheet**. Quotations from relevant sources (e.g., in independent school settings, from Aristotle, Plato, Horace, and other philosophers; in religiously affiliated school settings, from a holy scripture; in Montessori school settings, from Dr. Maria Montessori) serve to remind those who read your bylaws that a meaningful set of bylaws is a vehicle designed ultimately to promote a particular educational and/or spiritual point of view consistent with your school's mission.

- **Several pages displaying: (a) the institutional mission statement and (b) the current strategic plan**. Limit your mission statement to 30 words and your strategic plan to two or three pages. If your mission and strategic plan are of those lengths, they can easily be displayed in your bylaw document. If they are longer, then summaries could be provided. The next step is to begin linking your bylaws with your mission and plan in a strategic manner, distinct from a mere summarization of your institution's legal underpinnings. Having become strategic, they then become relevant in an entirely new way, helping Board leaders to fit structure and function to mission and plan.

- **Definitions**. A page that defines terms (e.g., Board, bylaws, Head, school, and other words/phrases to be used repeatedly in the document) provides an obvious opportunity to couch your bylaws in "strategic" terms. For example, "Board" may be defined as "the self-perpetuating entity charged with the strategic, longest-term protection and strengthening of the financial, physical, and programmatic assets of the institution." "Head" may be defined as "the institution's Chief Executive Officer and the Board's only employee." Definitions of this sort help to frame the Board's responsibilities strategically and in relationship to the school and to its Head.

- **Purposes and Powers**. A page devoted to statements of purpose and power can introduce the aforementioned "legal underpinnings" without diluting the strategic and philosophical thrust of the bylaws—e.g., "The school is organized exclusively for educational purposes within the context of Section 501(c)(3) of the United States Internal Revenue Service Code, or the corresponding provision of any future law of this nation." The school's "educational purposes" are those expressed in its institutional mission statement.

- **Board of Trustees** (Directors, Governors, etc.). This heading introduces the self-descriptive (structure and function) components of the detailed bylaws listing, and will display several subheads, such as the following.

Board-specific Stipulations

Powers. As the opening subhead under "Board of Trustees," this section should define the Board's legal and organizational capabilities more specifically than in the previous "Purposes and Powers" section. The language should reflect the centrality of the Board's strategic planning responsibilities. The following language is illustrative:

Subject to the provisions of the previous section ('Purposes and Powers'), all of the affairs and business of the school will be managed by the Board in a manner consistent with these bylaws and other applicable state and local constraints. The Board will focus on:

a. strategic planning and the annual agendas derived from the resulting planning document(s);

b. policy setting and policy implementation consistent with and pursuant to the planning document(s);

c. employment and evaluation of a School Head who will function as the Chief Executive Officer, on the Board's behalf, of the operations-level implementation of the planning document's component parts.

The Board will make appropriate delegations of authority to the Board's President and/or to the School Head and, to the extent permitted by law, by appropriate resolution the Board may authorize one or more Board committees to act on its behalf when it is not in session.

In addition to the general powers conferred by these bylaws, the specific powers of the Board will include, without limitation, the power to:

a. elect a President from among the Board members;

b. receive and hold by purchase, gift, etc., real or personal property for educational purposes connected with or for the benefit of the school;

c. develop and revise as needed both an overall strategic plan and a strategic financial plan derived therefrom, and, thus, to develop revenue sources and to establish expenditure systems consistent with the furtherance of the strategic plan and the strategic financial plan;

d. approve an annual budget consistent with the strategic financial plan;

e. fix the compensation package for the School Head;

f. having hired the School Head, either extend the School Head's contract in a systematic and timely manner or, in likewise manner, bring it to closure;

g. grant and confer diplomas (via the School Head and the faculty) to those completing the school's courses of study; and

h. amend these bylaws as necessary.

Number and Election of Trustees. The language of your bylaws—here and elsewhere—must be permissive, not prescriptive. Rather than, for example, specifying the number of Board members required, the bylaws should provide either a maximum number (e.g., "no more than 22 members") or a range (e.g., "17 to 22 members"). This approach allows the Board to make a strategic determination regarding the ideal number of Board members needed to carry out the planning document's implications at a given juncture.

This approach also allows the Board to avoid being forced by its own bylaws to fill seats with less-than-ideal new members. The following language is illustrative:

The Board of Trustees will consist of not less than 17 or more than 22 members. Subsequent to the recommendations of new members by the Committee on Trustees, all Trustees will be elected by the then-existing Board of Trustees by simple majority vote.

The guiding principle for the Committee on Trustees' recommendations, and for the full Board's subsequent approval, will be each (potential) new Trustee's willingness and capacity to further both the school's mission and its currently approved strategic plan.

Thus, the selection of new Trustees for your Board becomes part of the strategic school development process and is grounded in the language of the bylaw document itself.

- **Tenure of Trustees**. ISM recommends three-year terms that can be renewed once, followed by at least one (mandatory) year off the Board. However, "strategic" bylaws should include the stipulation that a Trustee appointment to a particular strategically focused responsibility be allowed to override this general (three-years-times-two) constraint. For example, if your Board President is elected at the start of her or his sixth year, then that six-year term should be extended to coincide with termination of the normal term served by Board Presidents in your school.

- **Meetings, Notice, Quorum, etc.** Boards should not stipulate in the bylaws a specific frequency of meetings, but simply state a minimum number of annual meetings (e.g., three) and include language to this effect:

  The Board President/Executive Committee will annually—normally during early summer—establish and publish the upcoming year's calendar of Board meetings as a function of the strategic plan's implications for the annual Board agenda. The primary rationale for establishing Board meeting dates will be the expected schedule of Board committee proposals to be discussed and voted upon. The primary rationale for committee proposal development will be the furtherance of the strategic plan. Thus, the Board meeting calendar will be annually designed in such a manner as to advance the strategic plan in the most efficient way possible.

- **Manner of Acting, Resignations and Removal, Proxies, Vacancies, Compensation, Procedure, Advisory Board, Conflict of Interest.** (The manner of acting may be formal or informal; proxies and compensation are prohibited.) "Strategic" bylaws differ little, if at all, from traditional bylaws in subsections such as these. If there is a perceptible difference, it is in the brevity and simplicity of strategic bylaws. They are designed to communicate in the most user-friendly fashion possible the basic strategic framework for Board structure/function. For example, one-sentence paragraphs such as "Proxies are not allowed" or "No Trustee will receive compensation for Board service" or "An Advisory Board may be formed or dissolved at any time by simple majority vote of the Board" are sufficient and complete as written.

Committees. "Strategic" bylaws emphasize the primacy of strategic process over the concept of standing committees. The following language illustrates this point:

> Committee structure and function will be determined annually by a process that begins with the Board President/Executive Committee's re-examination of the strategic plan (see previous Section on "Meetings, Notice, Quorum, etc."). This review, normally conducted each summer, results in the creation of the annual Board agenda—the schedule of actions to be taken in the upcoming year—followed by the determination of the exact committee structure most appropriate for fulfilling that agenda.

Having in such manner determined the committee structure and committee functions (i.e., committee charges for the year), the Board President/Executive Committee will select committee Chairs and, in consultation with the Chairs, develop lists of Trustees and non-Trustees to fill the roles in each committee with the individuals best suited to advance that committee's charge—and, thereby, the overall strategic plan—during the year.

Although this "strategic" approach mitigates against the concept of standing committees, five committees are likely to be renewed annually regardless of the exact Board agenda that is developed:

Executive Committee, Committee on Trustees, Head Support and Evaluation Committee, Finance Committee, and Development Committee with its subcommittees Annual Fund and Major Gifts.

The President/Executive Committee may then designate committees as needed to carry out the strategic plan.

Other Issues

- **Officers**. In a "strategic" approach to Board structure and function, the conventional array of officers often becomes a bureaucratic anachronism. A President is needed, certainly. Any responsibilities a Treasurer would handle can be reasonably discharged by the Chair of the Finance Committee. Minutes should be taken by a skilled clerical person, preferably the Administrative Assistant of a Trustee. The clerical person would be paid for his or her services by the Trustee, as a gift-in-kind to the institution. The following strategic bylaw language is illustrative:

The Board shall elect a President to serve a term the length of which shall be recommended by the Committee on Trustees, that Committee having examined the strategic plan and the (prospective or newly elected) President's qualifications to lead the Board through the plan's various stages.

The Board Treasurer's functions, if any, shall be discharged by the Chair of the Finance Committee.

Board minutes shall be recorded, transcribed, and circulated by a qualified clerical person hired to perform these duties with great discretion. That individual shall not be otherwise employed by the school or related by marriage or birth to any employee of the school.

In the President's absence, the Chair of the Finance Committee shall preside.

- **Duties of the President**. The President's duties, in addition to the obvious one of presiding at Board meetings, are summarized in the foregoing section titled "Committees."

- **Duties of the School Head**. While the Head's role has been defined briefly elsewhere in this document, a separate section may be useful. The following language is illustrative:

  The School Head, the Board's only employee, will be the Chief Executive Officer of all school operations. Subject to the ultimate authority of the Board, the School Head will supervise and control all of the business and affairs of the institution with no Board-level interference (except when Board involvement in operations may be explicitly requested by the Head to assist in a particular exigency, and except for Head Support and Evaluation Committee activity).

  The Head will, in particular, advance the institution's Board-approved strategic plan and that plan's financial subset, the strategic financial plan, at the operations level, and will be held accountable for doing so by means of the Head Support and Evaluation Committee of the Board.

  The Head, although not a member of the Board, will be present at all full-Board meetings save any during which the Head's performance or compensation is under review. (The Head may or may not be invited to be present during such review.)

  The Head's role within the Board committee structure (aside from Head Support and Evaluation Committee meetings at which the Head will by definition always be present) will be dictated by the implications of the annual Board and operations agendas. However, the Head's presence at meetings of the Executive Committee, Committee on Trustees, and Major Gifts/Annual Fund (Sub)Committees will normally be "strategic," regardless of the details of the two agendas in a given year.

- **Contracts, Gifts, Fiscal Year Defined, Indemnification, Amendments.** These subsections will be displayed in "strategic" bylaws just as they are in conventional approaches to bylaw construction. Regardless of a Board's strategic orientation (or not), bylaws need paragraphs authorizing the

Board's and the institution's entry into contractual agreements, authorizing the receipt of gifts in all forms (monetary and other), specifying the institution's fiscal year, indemnifying the Board and its members in all good-faith actions and transactions, and specifying the process of amending the bylaws.

Committee Summaries in Bylaws

As you develop or reconsider your bylaws, your Board committees should be well defined. The following wording is illustrative:

> The core structure and function of the five "strategic" committees may be summarized as follows:
>
> **Executive Committee**. An Executive Committee of Board members may be selected by the Board President to have and exercise, when the Board is not in session and prudent management requires prompt action, all of the authority of the Board in the governance of the school, except as such authority is limited by resolution of the Board and specifically except for alteration of the mission statement, purchase or sale of property, or the hiring or firing of the Head, each of which requires full-Board action regardless of circumstances. Such "emergency" actions of the Executive Committee will be reported at the next meeting of the Board for action in accordance with the Board's direction.
>
> The Executive Committee will set the Head's compensation, having first received the annual report of the Head Support and Evaluation Committee, and having consulted with the Chair of the Finance Committee.
>
> The Executive Committee will serve as a Board management unit, annually reviewing the strategic plan, determining the annual Board agenda, developing committee structure/function, selecting committee leadership, and, with that leadership, determining committee membership and overseeing committees' progress toward their agreed-upon charges. Given the clustering of the Executive Committee's work in the summer months, its members are free to hold leadership (and other) roles on other committees—except the Committee on Trustees—throughout the year.

Committee on Trustees. A Committee on Trustees may be formed for the purposes and activities listed as following:

1. The Committee on Trustees will periodically review the strategic plan to ascertain the Board's personnel needs—professional "mix," financial "mix," and other—in upcoming years.
2. The Committee on Trustees will then profile the Board, listing the ideal characteristics implicit in the most appropriate "mix" of members needed for the fulfillment of the strategic plan's goals (e.g., expertise in finance, land development, non-profit marketing, non-profit management, plant maintenance, and access to a variety of affluence networks).
3. The Committee on Trustees will then identify individuals whose characteristics and backgrounds (cumulatively) fulfill the profile.
4. The Committee on Trustees will then formulate a cultivation plan to bring those individuals to eventual Board (and/or Board committee) membership.
5. The Committee on Trustees will oversee the cultivation process.
6. The Committee on Trustees will, at the appropriate time, nominate cultivated individuals for Board and/or Board committee membership.
7. The Committee on Trustees will devise and implement an annual Board orientation session(s) for the newly elected members
8. The Committee on Trustees will conduct an evaluation of the Board on (at least) an annual basis. This evaluation will be based upon the level of excellence with which the Board will have met its annual Board agenda. The evaluation will focus upon the Board's overall success, but will include individuals and individual committees (including the Board President and the Executive Committee), as needed and as appropriate. The objective of the evaluation will be the ongoing strengthening of the Board.

Since the Committee on Trustees "balances the power" within the Board's internal structure, its Chair and composition will not be determined by the Board President and/or Executive Committee, but by whole-Board election. (The Committee on Trustees may choose to recommend to the whole Board its own successors in the same way that it may choose to recommend to the President/Executive Committee other committee leadership and membership positions.)

Head Support and Evaluation Committee. A Head Support and Evaluation Committee may be appointed by the Board President/ Executive Committee in order to discharge the Board's responsibility to ensure the strategic plan's advancement at the operations level.

The Head Evaluation Committee will work in concert with the School Head to delineate several annual major objectives, each of which clearly advances the strategic plan and/or corrects an operations-level weakness or problem.

The Head Evaluation Committee will be comprised of no more than five members, a minority of whom may be requested by the School Head, and all of whom qualify as capable mentors/advisers for the Head. A minority may be non-Board members.

Finance Committee. A Finance Committee may be appointed by the Board President/Executive Committee in order to develop the details of a strategic financial plan (a subset of the overall strategic plan), and to develop and recommend to the full Board an annual operations budget that will conform to, and efficiently advance, the strategic plan and its financial components. The Chair of the Finance Committee will act as Board Treasurer if and when that function is required.

Development Committee. A Development Committee may be appointed by the Board President/Executive Committee in order to develop the details of an overall external affairs and institutional advancement framework consistent with, and in furtherance of, the strategic plan. As circumstances warrant, the annual fund and major gifts programs may be organized under separate subcommittees, reporting to the Development Committee.

Trustee Workbook

Name: ______________________

School: ______________________

Year: ______________________

Committee: __________________

Committee: __________________

Section 1: Mission Comparisons

Instructions: This section invites you to be thoughtful, at least once per year, about the school's reason-for-being, your own reason-for-being in that context, and the congruence (or not) between the two.

School mission. Please write the school mission statement or, alternatively, phrases from the mission/philosophy/core values on which you expect to concentrate most forcefully and thoughtfully in the upcoming school year.

____

____

____

____

____

Personal/professional mission. Write into the space below a concise summary of your own reason-for-being as a school Trustee.

____

____

____

____

____

Comparison/contrast. Examine the two statements above. With marginal notes, circles, arrows, or other indicators, highlight any especially congruent or incongruent ideas or phrases. Note below the possible impact of these items on your agenda for the upcoming school year.

Section 2: Trustee Self-rating

Instructions: Self-ratings. Following is a list of Trustee leadership/management characteristics. Rate yourself on each of the 14 items. Nine represents the "high" end of the scale. Once you have gone through the items, use the comment section at the end to reflect on how you see your own performance and what you would like to emphasize in the coming year.

Don't take on more than two areas to really work at improving. Chances are you won't do it. Pick your one or two items and decide what you want to do about them. For example, you may have scored yourself low on No. 1 (vigorously pursue my own professional growth ...) and determine to make attending the summer Board retreat and the workshop offered in the fall a high priority. Or you may have scored yourself low on No. 4 (demonstrate strategic thinking and oppose "current parent" thinking) and determine only to engage with agenda items at meetings in the future, rather than bringing up current affairs topics that are not part of the actual agenda.

As a Trustee for my school, I ...

1. Vigorously pursue my own professional growth in being a Trustee and encourage my fellow Trustees to do the same

   1 2 3 4 5 6 7 8 9

2. Show respect for others regardless of their position in the organization

   1 2 3 4 5 6 7 8 9

3. Consistently display "muted charisma" (i.e., a "strong personality" dampened by humility)

   1 2 3 4 5 6 7 8 9

4. Demonstrate strategic thinking and oppose "current parent" thinking

   1 2 3 4 5 6 7 8 9

5. Carry out my Trustee due diligence (meeting attendance, etc.)

   1 2 3 4 5 6 7 8 9

6. Am seen as being steeped in moral purpose, clarity, conviction, and integrity

   1 2 3 4 5 6 7 8 9

7. Am seen as student-centered

   1 2 3 4 5 6 7 8 9

8. Display predictability (i.e., display consistency in my responses to others)

   1 2 3 4 5 6 7 8 9

9. Display supportiveness (i.e., display the attitude of being on the side of the Administration, faculty, and staff even when I am in disagreement)

   1 2 3 4 5 6 7 8 9

10. Give public positive reinforcement consistently

    1 2 3 4 5 6 7 8 9

11. Give financially at the level that I know I am capable of whenever asked

    1 2 3 4 5 6 7 8 9

12. Am seen as being self-aware, and as being effective at self-management (i.e., I am seen as someone who both monitors her/his behaviors and then modifies those behaviors as appropriate in order to be organizationally effective and to remain physically and mentally healthy)

    1 2 3 4 5 6 7 8 9

13. Am seen as displaying an inspired and inspirational commitment to the school mission

    1 2 3 4 5 6 7 8 9

14. Carry out my committee duties very conscientiously

    1 2 3 4 5 6 7 8 9

Comment section (choose one or two items and plan what you will do to improve). The Committee on Trustees will hold you accountable for this!

Item: ____

Plan: ____

____

____

____

Item: ____

Plan: ____

____

____

____

Note: If you are falling down on your duties in, for example, No. 14, the Committee on Trustees may encourage you to include that as one of your items.

Section 3: Trustee Leadership/Management Agenda

Instructions: Fill out this sheet. There is space for only two committees. Do not commit to more than two and preferably only one. You need to do your job at a level of excellence. You are a volunteer. Don't set the school up for disappointment. There is a success comment so that you can write down the level of success you and your committee achieved at the end of your process. At the end of each year, this sheet will become part of your Trustee file held by the Committee on Trustees.

Committee #1: ____

Committee charge: ____

____

____

____

____

My responsibilities:____

____

____

____

____

Date the Committee is due to make its recommendation for action:

____

Success Comment: ____

____

Signed: ______________________

Print Name: ______________________

Date: ______________________

Committee #2: ____

Committee charge: ____

____

____

____

____

My responsibilities:______________________________________

____

____

____

____

Date the Committee is due to make its recommendation for action:

____

Success Comment: ____

____

Signed: ______________________

Print Name: ______________________

Date: ______________________

Section 4: Revisions, Discussions, Comments

Instructions: Annotate during the year to ensure that there is regular feedback, collection of data, provision of support, modification as necessary, and discussion of issues surrounding this document.

More ISM Publications

School Leaders

The Tuition Book: Theory, Implementation, and Financial Aid

Leadership & Change: Perspectives for the School Head

Policies & Procedures for Private-Independent Schools

The Business Manager's Guide: Risk Management, Human Resources, and Insurance

Marketing

Marketing Your School: Theory, Planning, and Strategy

Marketing Your School: Recruiting and Re-recruiting Families

Marketing Your School: In Print, On Air, and Online

Faculty Professional Development

MFE: Faculty Development & Renewal™ Implementer's Guide

MFE: Faculty Development & Renewal™ Reference Book

The Teacher's Professional Growth Workbook

Twenty Principles for Teaching Excellence: The Teacher's Workbook

Mission-Based Advisory: A Professional Development Manual

School Leadership and Management Evaluation

ISM's Strategic Board Evaluation

ISM's Xcellence in Executive Leadership™ (XEL): A School Head Evaluation Instrument

ISM's Xcellence in Executive Leadership™ (XEL): A Management Team Evaluation Instrument

ISM's Xcellence in Executive Leadership™ (XEL): A Support Staff Evaluation Instrument

Advisory Letters

Ideas & Perspectives

To The Point

isminc.com/bookstore